BELOVED

This is YOUR year to create.
Make it an AMAZING year,
using your intuition and your
Tarot cards as a guide.

ACKNOWLEDGEMENTS

I am so proud to share the 2022 Biddy Tarot Planner with you! Of course, it would not have been possible without the help of some very special humans.

My deepest gratitude to Tássia Assis for designing the layout of the Biddy Tarot Planner; Anthony Esselmont for designing the front and back covers; MJ Valentine for joining forces with me to co-create the New and Full Moon spreads, and writing the monthly astrological influences and crystal profiles; Team Biddy for editing the planner, making it sparkle, and bringing it to life; and the whole Biddy Tarot community for your ongoing love and support. Together, we have created something amazing, and I truly hope you love it!

The Tarot deck featured in the 2022 Biddy Tarot Planner is the Lumina Tarot, republished with permission from the author, Lauren Aletta, from Inner Hue. The Lumina Tarot is available for sale via www.biddytarot.com/lumina.

Note: The exact date of lunations may vary depending on your region. This planner was made using US Pacific time. To know the exact dates for your region, go to www.timeanddate.com/moon/phases.

WELCOME

Welcome to 2022: The Year of Conscious Connections

If you've been craving more depth in your relationships and a more intentional and soulFULL way of living — this is your year! A potent and exciting year, filled with endless opportunities to develop conscious connections is ahead of you. And the good news is, bringing your vision to life this year will be even more possible now that you've said "yes" to your intuition and partnered with this Planner.

With the Biddy Tarot Planner by your side, you'll tune in to your Higher Self, manifest your goals and dreams, and create a life that is in full alignment with your soul's purpose — all while using Tarot as your guide.

The Biddy Tarot Planner will empower you to:

⊚ Tap into the collective energy of each month with the intuitive Tarot forecast

⊚ Use monthly rituals to deepen your connection with the collective energy

⊚ Explore the blessings of each New and Full Moon

⊚ Create personalized daily forecasts to maximize the potential of each day

⊚ Complete seasonal Tarot spreads and connect with what each stage of the upcoming year has in store for you

This Planner has been designed to help you create an amazing year ahead, learn to trust your intuition, and allow the Tarot cards to guide you to your most deeply fulfilling year yet.

So, get out your favorite Tarot deck, grab your crystals, uncap your best markers, and prepare to get up close and personal with your divine power.

Lots of love and success,

[signature]

P.S.

We love celebrating our community — and that means you! Don't forget to share LOTS of photos and videos of your Planner on Instagram, using the hashtag **#biddytarotplanner**.

Make sure you're following **@biddytarot**, as we'll be sharing even more tips to help you use Tarot to create your year of Conscious Connections.

FREE BONUS [VALUE $197]
BIDDY TAROT PLANNER TOOLKIT

To help you achieve your highest potential and get the most out of your 2022 Biddy Tarot Planner, I've created a free bonus Toolkit, including:

6 incredible video tutorials to set you up for success by showing you how to make the most of your planner, diving in-depth into the 2022 Card Of The Year, the New Year's Ritual, Seasonal Spreads, Lunar Spreads, and more!

3 powerful meditations to help you harness the lunar universal energy regularly, including one for the New Moon and one for the Full Moon, PLUS an extra special bonus meditation to tune into the energy of the Card of the Year.

A guide to navigating Mercury Retrograde and a special Mercury Retrograde Tarot spread to keep you balanced and prepared for anything.

Print-your-own Tarot cards to use inside of the Planner.

4 deep-dive Tarot spreads for self-discovery, spiritual advancement, and trusting your intuition.

Detailed guidance on how to use the Daily Tarot Card practice.

And so much more!

DOWNLOAD THE FREE PLANNER TOOLKIT AT
WWW.BIDDYTAROT.COM/2022-PLANNER-BONUS

TABLE OF CONTENTS

HOW TO MAKE THE MOST OUT OF YOUR PLANNER

To get started, here's what you will need:

- ⊙ Your favorite Tarot deck
- ⊙ Your favorite markers, pens, and pencils
- ⊙ Your free Bonus Planner Toolkit (download it at www.biddytarot.com/2022-planner-bonus)

> If you're on Instagram, I would love to see your Tarot spreads! Use the hashtag **#biddytarotplanner** to post your photos of the Planner and your readings, and we'll share them with the Biddy Tarot community!

Here's how to create your Year of Conscious Connection with the Biddy Tarot Planner:

FIRST, WATCH THE VIDEO TUTORIALS

I've created a series of tutorial videos to show you how to make the most of the Biddy Tarot Planner. I'll be there with you every step of the way!

For free access, go to www.biddytarot.com/2022-planner-bonus.

AT THE START OF THE YEAR...

Start your year with the **New Year's Ritual** (on page 16) — a divine experience of self-reflection, intuitive journaling, and Tarot card consultation.

And connect with the energy of the **2022 Tarot card — the Lovers**. Take some time to reflect on what its energy means for you as you step into the new year.

FOR EACH SEASON...

At the start of each season, you'll be invited to do a **Seasonal Tarot Spread** to explore the energy of the season and use that energy to set your goals and intentions for the upcoming three months.

A note on location: The seasons in this Planner have been designed for those in the Northern Hemisphere. If you are in the Southern Hemisphere, please swap the seasons so you're doing the Summer Tarot Spread in December, and so on.

AT THE START OF THE MONTH...

Reflect on the insights I've shared for each monthly Tarot card. Then take it to the next level by connecting with what that card means for you. Ask how you can harness this energy and use it throughout the month ahead.

Next, do the **ritual** associated with the Tarot card. You may do the ritual just once during the month or more frequently. You can also continue to use the ritual again in the following months if you feel called to do so.

Each month you will also find a recommended **crystal** to help you connect more deeply with that month's Tarot card. You could carry the crystal with you throughout the month, wear it, place it on your desk or in your bedroom, or even bring it out each time you do a Tarot reading — be creative!

Finally, I've noted some of the major **astrological influences** that are at play during the month, so your cards and stars align.

While we're speaking about planetary influences — keep an eye out for Mercury Retrograde, which occurs four times this year. Renowned for wreaking havoc with communication, timing, travel, and technology, it's a good idea to avoid activities such as signing contracts, launching products, and making technical upgrades during this Retrograde.

But it's not all bad! During Mercury Retrograde, it's also the perfect time for most "re" activities: reflection, reassessment, revisiting the past, reworking or closing out a project, and re-evaluating your priorities.

For each Mercury Retrograde of the year, you can complete the **Mercury Retrograde Tarot Spread** (inside the Tarot Reader's Survival Guide to Mercury Retrograde, in your Toolkit) to gain clarity through this potentially confusing time. Grab it here: www.biddytarot.com/2022-planner-bonus.

FOR EACH DAY...

At the beginning of each day, draw a Tarot card and set your intention for the day ahead. Note your card and thoughts in the planner. At the end of the day, reflect on what you have learned and discovered based on the energy of your daily card.

For more ideas on how to do the daily Tarot card draw, check out www.biddytarot.com/daily-tarot-card.

ON THE NEW MOON AND THE FULL MOON...

Without question, the cycles of the Moon have an impact on our own personal cycles. For each New and Full Moon, do the spread that corresponds to the astrological sign of the Moon.

Reminder: On the **New Moon**, set your intentions for the next two weeks and get ready to start new projects and make way for new beginnings. On the **Full Moon**, give thanks for what you have achieved and manifested over the past two weeks, and let go of what is no longer serving you. Don't forget to clear and cleanse your energy and your space during this time. I've created a special New Moon and Full Moon Ritual *plus* two guided visualizations so you can fully tap into the power of the lunar cycles. Access them in the Toolkit here: www.biddytarot.com/2022-planner-bonus.

A note on timing: All times and dates of the lunar cycles are in US Pacific time.

IF YOU NEED A LITTLE HELP WITH THE TAROT CARD MEANINGS...

To make the most out of the Biddy Tarot Planner, all you need is a basic knowledge of the Tarot cards — your intuition will take care of the rest! However, I know you may also want a little extra guidance along the way — so I have two helpful resources for you:

[BOOK] THE ULTIMATE GUIDE TO TAROT CARD MEANINGS

In this modern guide to the Tarot card meanings, you'll discover how to interpret the cards in your Tarot readings with ease. An Amazon best-seller, *The Ultimate Guide to Tarot Card Meanings* includes:

⊘ Detailed descriptions of the 78 Tarot cards, including upright and reversed meanings

⊘ What each card means in relationship, work, finance, spiritual, and well-being readings.

This is a must-have reference guide for all Tarot readers, from beginners to professionals, to help you quickly and easily decipher the meaning of your Tarot readings. Buy the book at www.biddytarot.com/guide.

MASTER THE TAROT CARD MEANINGS

[ONLINE COURSE] MASTER THE TAROT CARD MEANINGS

My program, Master the Tarot Card Meanings, is the #1 online Tarot training course to help you instantly and intuitively interpret the 78 cards in the Tarot deck — without memorization.

In Master the Tarot Card Meanings, I'll show you how to build a unique personal connection with the Tarot, using simple yet powerful techniques for interpreting the cards. Plus, you'll learn the 'must know' systems within the Tarot to make learning the card meanings super simple.

Together, we'll walk through all 78 Tarot cards, so you can master each and every one of them once and for all!

Learn more at www.biddytarot.com/mtcm or start with our free training at www.biddytarot.com/webinar-mtcm.

AND LASTLY, REMEMBER...

⊘ To make the most out of this Planner, check out my free video tutorials and bonuses at www.biddytarot.com/2022-planner-bonus.

⊘ Post photos of your Planner and Tarot spreads to Instagram with the hashtag #biddytarotplanner to get a shout-out!

WANT TO GET STARTED EARLY?

⊘ Download the Planner pages for October, November, and December 2021 (for free!) at www.biddytarot.com/2022-planner-bonus so that you can get started right now!

2021 REFLECTION

As we come to the end of 2021, take some time to reflect on the past 12 months and prepare yourself for the year to come.

For each question, journal your intuitive thoughts first, then if you feel called to do so, draw a Tarot card to help you go deeper.

1. What were my biggest achievements for 2021?

2. What were my biggest challenges for 2021?

3. How have I developed as a person?

4. What did I learn in 2021?

5. How would I describe 2021 in just three words?

6. What aspects of 2021 can I leave behind?

7. What aspects of 2021 can I bring with me into 2022?

8. What seeds of opportunity are being planted?

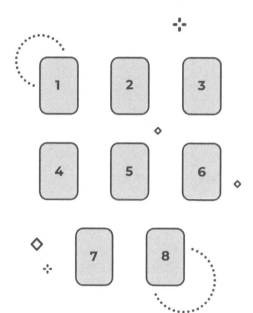

1. WHAT WERE MY BIGGEST ACHIEVEMENTS FOR 2021?

Don't forget to snap a pic of your reading and share on IG using the hashtag **#biddytarotplanner**. We love seeing you using your Biddy Tarot Planner in action and can't wait to celebrate with you!

2021 REFLECTION | 9

2. WHAT WERE MY BIGGEST CHALLENGES FOR 2021?

3. HOW HAVE I DEVELOPED AS A PERSON?

4. WHAT DID I LEARN IN 2021?

5. HOW WOULD I DESCRIBE 2021 IN JUST THREE WORDS?

6. WHAT ASPECTS OF 2021 CAN I LEAVE BEHIND?

7. WHAT ASPECTS OF 2021 CAN I BRING WITH ME INTO 2022?

8. WHAT SEEDS OF OPPORTUNITY ARE BEING PLANTED?

2022

2022

At its core, this card — and this year — is about honoring the Highest Good within yourself and others, creating meaningful relationships, and making conscious, empowered choices. This is a potent year for expanding your impact, reaching your highest potential, and of course, creating conscious connections with yourself, your loved ones, and your community.

The Lovers, despite the name, is not exclusively about romantic relationships. The energy of The Lovers allows you to cultivate deep, meaningful, and awakened relationships — also known as conscious connections — with yourself, your loved ones, your community, and everything you interact with and invite into your life.

And it all starts with you...

Just as The Lovers are personified by two beings, you are called to embrace your own duality and to love and accept yourself for who you truly are. Light and shade, good and bad, ugly and beautiful — this card invites you to fall madly in love with it all. As you step into 2022, know that your true power is not in denying your weaknesses and only focusing on your strengths. Instead, it is welcoming all parts of yourself and giving yourself a healthy dose of self-love, compassion, and kindness. Because when you truly love and accept yourself, it will inevitably radiate out into the world.

By cultivating self-love, you'll see the Highest Good in others too.

Your invitation this year is to create fulfilling connections with those around you. Look to people who light you up and raise your vibration and invest in these relationships. But also look to those people who may trigger or challenge you in certain ways. These relationships are here to serve you and reflect back to you what you need to accept within yourself. Respond from a place of love and embrace each other's differences, knowing that you have a beautiful opportunity to learn and grow.

Your conscious connections expand beyond your immediate environment — they reach far and wide to the global community.

The Lovers card asks, "What impact are you having in your community? How are you consciously engaging with those around you and beyond? Are you raising global awareness? What more can you be doing?" Whether it's the environment, animals, overcoming poverty, helping to end homelessness, expanding cultural awareness, or another issue close to your heart, you are invited this year to follow your desire to make the world a better place while also honoring the platforms of others. The Lovers invites you to choose the high road and make your world a better place this year. Empower yourself and others to make the conscious choice to join (or start!) a movement that aligns with your values.

Finally, this is a year for clarity of your desires and your values.

The Lovers will urge you to become clear on who you want to be in this lifetime, how you connect with others and on what level, and what you will and won't stand for. Remember that The Lovers card is often a sign you are facing a moral dilemma and must consider all consequences before acting. To make powerful choices, you'll need to be crystal clear on your personal beliefs and values — and most importantly, stay true to them. It may not always be easy to take the higher path (it rarely is) but this year, now, more than ever, you must choose love — for yourself, for others, for the Universe. And by choosing love, you are choosing the best version of yourself too.

RITUAL: OPENING THE HEART

Find a quiet place where you won't be disturbed. Take out The Lovers card and reflect on its energy. Notice the imagery, colors, and symbols that stand out to you today. Then, when you're ready, light a candle, and burn some rose or ylang ylang oil.

Close your eyes and connect with the energetic center of your heart, your heart chakra. Visualize a ball of pink light radiating from your heart. Feel the light growing and expanding as it first fills your body, then begins to radiate out into your aura, your room, your neighborhood, and eventually into the world and Universe beyond. Take a moment to feel this deep, radiant love that you have both created and tapped into.

Finally, say this affirmation 3 times: "I honor the love inside me and connect consciously with others." When you're ready, open your eyes and journal your experience.

JOURNALING PROMPTS

Use these journaling prompts throughout the year to help you stay in alignment with The Lovers energy.

- How can I create conscious connections...
  - With myself?
  - With my loved ones?
  - With my community?
- What aspects of my own duality (the light and the shade) am I currently denying?
- How can I best acknowledge and embrace the aspects of myself I currently perceive as weaknesses?
- What are the core values and ethics that influence major choices in my life?

REFLECT BACK ON 2013 — THE MOST RECENT YEAR OF THE LOVERS

- What conscious connections did I create and nurture in 2013?

- How have those connections evolved?

- What have I discovered about myself and my relationships with others along the way?

INSIGHTS

NEW YEAR'S RITUAL

This New Year's Ritual is a beautiful, empowering way to start the new year! You'll be connecting with your Higher Self and envisioning what you truly want to manifest in the year to come. This is about positive change and transformation at a deep, symbolic level that will help you to create an abundant, super-charged year ahead!

I encourage you to use this ritual as a guide only. Rituals become even more powerful when **you** create them, so use this as a starting point and then get creative with what you want to include.

Ready? Let's do it!

STEP 1: CREATE YOUR SACRED SPACE

Gather everything you need for the ritual and begin to create your sacred space.

Next, set up your altar. Your altar doesn't have to be super fancy. Simply use items that represent what you want to manifest in 2022. You can include crystals, Tarot cards, jewelry, flowers, rocks — whatever helps you to create a sacred intention for your ritual.

Place the candles in and around your altar. When you're all set up and ready, switch off the lights, and light the candles.

Take a moment to ground yourself. Close your eyes and take in a few deep breaths. Connect in with the Earth energy and the Universal energy, feeling yourself filled with a beautiful white light.

STEP 2: REFLECT ON THE PAST YEAR

Reflect on the year that was 2021. What did you experience? What were the highs? What were the lows? And what did you learn along the way?

To support you in this process, use the New Year's Tarot Spread on page 20. Draw the first 2 cards and write your insights in the spaces provided on pages 20 and 21.

Then, write your thoughts about the past year on the next page.

BEFORE YOU START, YOU WILL NEED...

- ⊙ Your Biddy Tarot Planner

- ⊙ Your favorite Tarot deck — the Everyday Tarot Deck is a great place to start (available via www.everydaytarot.com/deck)

- ⊙ Your favorite markers

- ⊙ At least one candle and some matches

- ⊙ An herbal bundle for clearing and cleansing

- ⊙ Items for your altar. These are symbols of what you want to create in 2022, such as an image of your ideal relationship, a flower for beauty, a seed pod for starting something new — you choose!

- ⊙ At least one hour of uninterrupted time — lock the door, turn off your phone, do whatever you need to protect your sacred space

- ⊙ (Optional) Your favorite crystals — I recommend citrine for abundance and clear quartz for clarity

- ⊙ The New Year's Tarot Spread (page 20)

Remember, if you would like extra guidance for the New Year's Ritual, watch the free video tutorials at www.biddytarot.com/2022-planner-bonus

Take the herbal bundle and light it. Then, wave the smoke around your body, front and back, as you cleanse your aura and release any old energy that may be clinging to you. For each item on your list, say aloud, "I release myself of... {insert what you want to release}."

When you feel complete, say aloud three times, **"I give thanks for the past year. I release what no longer serves me. And I welcome new opportunities with open arms."**

STEP 3: VISUALIZE WHAT YOU WANT TO CREATE IN 2022

Now, close your eyes and start to imagine what you want to create in 2022.

Think about what you want to create in your relationships. Then, play out what that would look like in your head, as if you were watching a movie. See yourself in that movie as an active participant in fulfilling, loving relationships. What do you see, hear, feel, taste, smell? Create a full sensory experience.

When you're ready, wipe the movie screen clean, and bring up a new movie, this time about your career, work and finances. What do you want to create in your material world?

When you're complete, bring up the next movie for your health and well-being. And after that, your personal development. What do you want to create?

When you feel complete, open your eyes, and write down your experiences on the next page.

Next, take out your Tarot cards and continue with Cards 3 to 9 of the New Year's Tarot Spread. Write your cards and insights in the space provided on pages 21 to 23.

RELATIONSHIPS

HEALTH AND WELL-BEING

CAREER AND FINANCES

PERSONAL DEVELOPMENT

STEP 4: MANIFEST YOUR GOALS FOR 2022

Read over your insights from Step 3 and choose 10 things you want to manifest in 2022 (e.g. I want to be fit and healthy, or I want to take a 3-month vacation).

Then, change these to "I am" statements (yes, even if they sound a little funny). For example, "I AM fit and healthy" or "I AM enjoying a 3-month vacation." Take a moment to feel the energy and the vibration of these "I am" statements — super powerful, right?!

Now, complete your New Year Tarot Spread from Cards 10 to 12 and write your cards and insights in the spaces provided on pages 23 and 24.

Finally, close your eyes and visualize the energy of what you want to create as a bright white light. Imagine it as a ball of light radiating within your solar plexus (just above your belly button). Then imagine the ball of light getting bigger and bigger, filling your body, flowing through your aura, and illuminating out into the world. This is your power, your determination, your ability to manifest your goals, just as you see them. When you are ready, gently open your eyes.

STEP 5: CLOSE THE SPACE

Before you close the space, check in with your Higher Self and ask if there is anything else that needs to be done before this ritual is complete. Sometimes your intuition may guide you towards another sacred activity before you know for sure that you are done.

When you're ready, say a prayer of thanks to your Higher Self for guiding you along this process. Then, say out loud, "And so it is."

Blow out the candles, turn on the lights, then pack up the space. You may wish to leave part of your altar there or move it somewhere more convenient, so you have a visual reminder of this beautiful ritual that you have gifted yourself.

INSIGHTS

NEW YEAR'S TAROT SPREAD

Gain the clarity you need for your Year of Conscious Connections with the New Year's Tarot Spread. This is a powerful spread to use at the start of the year. Or, use it on your birthday to gain valuable insight into what you might experience during your next year of life.

1. The previous year in summary

2. Lessons learned from the past year

3. Aspirations for the next 12 months

4. What empowers you in reaching your aspirations

5. What may stand in the way of reaching your aspirations

6. Your relationships and emotions in the coming year

7. Your career, work, and finances

8. Your health and well-being

9. Your spiritual energy and inner fulfillment

10. What you most need to focus on in the year ahead

11. Your most important lesson for the coming year

12. Overall, where you are headed in the next 12 months

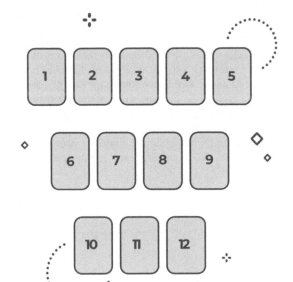

1. THE PREVIOUS YEAR IN SUMMARY

Excited with what 2022 might bring you? Post a pic of your spread using the hashtag **#biddytarotplanner** and we'll share with the Biddy Tarot community!

2. LESSONS LEARNED FROM THE PAST YEAR

3. ASPIRATIONS FOR THE NEXT 12 MONTHS

4. WHAT EMPOWERS YOU IN REACHING YOUR ASPIRATIONS

5. WHAT MAY STAND IN THE WAY OF REACHING YOUR ASPIRATIONS

6. YOUR RELATIONSHIPS AND EMOTIONS IN THE COMING YEAR

7. YOUR CAREER, WORK, AND FINANCES

8. YOUR HEALTH AND WELL-BEING

9. YOUR SPIRITUAL ENERGY AND INNER FULFILLMENT

10. WHAT YOU MOST NEED TO FOCUS ON IN THE YEAR AHEAD

11. YOUR MOST IMPORTANT LESSON FOR THE COMING YEAR

12. OVERALL, WHERE YOU ARE HEADED IN THE NEXT 12 MONTHS

JANUARY

THE DEVIL

What are you attached to? The Devil invites you to consider what you can release so you can align with the new, expansive energy of 2022. Take this opportunity to clear negative thought patterns, limiting beliefs, and unhealthy habits. Tune into what you truly desire in your life, and make changes accordingly. But be aware: The Devil also offers a powerful contrast to the Card of the Year — The Lovers. Where The Lovers calls you to make good, moral choices, you may find The Devil pulls you in the opposite direction. Resist the temptation to take the easy path — it may bring satisfaction in the short-term, but discontent in the long run.

 ## RITUAL: TRANSFORMATION AND REBIRTH

Find The Devil in your Tarot deck and place it in front of you. Spend some time drawing in the energy of this card and listening to the messages it has for you. In your journal, write down all of your unhealthy attachments and negative patterns. When you feel this list is complete, close your eyes, and bring yourself into a state of reflective relaxation. Imagine you're holding a beautiful selenite wand. Feel the intensity of its power, and begin making slicing motions around your body. With each strike, imagine you're snipping any negative energy cords that may still be attached to you, freeing yourself from their effects. In your mind's eye, wave the wand over the front and back of your body, over your head and under your feet. Continue until you feel complete, freeing yourself of the negativity, and then open your eyes when you feel ready.

 ## CRYSTAL: SELENITE

Selenite is a powerful stone known for clearing energy and purifying energetic space. It's used in the ritual above to cut cords and release the unhealthy energetic attachments of the Devil. It's the perfect stone to ring in a brand new year! Allow selenite to bring clarity and pure intentions for the month of January.

 ## ASTROLOGICAL INFLUENCES

January 1 | Mercury into Aquarius: Original ideas abound. This offbeat energy is perfect for inventive problem-solving and challenging the status quo. Try not to critique or criticize others too harshly; everyone's view is valid.

January 14–February 3 | Mercury Retrograde: Utilize the Tarot Reader's Survival Guide for Mercury Retrograde inside of your Toolkit at www.biddytarot.com/2022-planner-bonus to help navigate through this time.

January 19 | Happy Aquarius Season!
Idealism, individualism, innovation, spontaneity, independence.

INSIGHTS

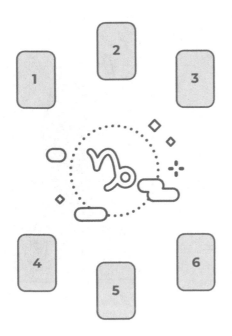

JANUARY 2
NEW MOON IN CAPRICORN

The first New Moon of the year falls in Capricorn, which rules stability, structure, and goals. It's a great time to work on a solid plan that will bring your dreams to life in the new year.

1. What insights did I gain in 2021 around what I want to achieve in 2022?

2. Which areas of my life might benefit from creating a sense of order?

3. How can I best support my financial goals this year?

4. What goals do I want to achieve within the next six months?

5. What kind of structure do I need to establish to support those goals?

6. Which grounding practices would best support me this year?

INSIGHTS

JANUARY 17

FULL MOON IN CANCER

If there was ever a time to release any feelings that you're holding onto day-to-day, the Full Moon in Cancer is the time. Dive into your emotional world and set empowering intentions around what feelings you want to release.

1. What new feelings are coming up for me right now that need to be released?

2. Where do I need to empower myself to be more vulnerable in my relationships?

3. How might I benefit from setting boundaries?

4. How can I level-up my self-care practice?

5. What do I need to know about creating sacred space in my home?

6. What new approach can I take to support my emotional well-being?

INSIGHTS

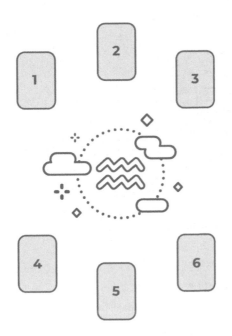

JANUARY 31

NEW MOON IN AQUARIUS

An Aquarius New Moon is an opportunity to set out-of-the-box intentions — make your plans according to what you really want, not what other people think or expect.

1. What unique gifts do I bring to the table?

2. How can I best utilize these gifts for the betterment of humanity?

3. Where would I most like to see social change and equality?

4. How am I best placed to communicate my ideas with the world?

5. How can I connect with others who align with my vision for the future?

6. Which areas of my life would benefit from expressing vulnerability?

INSIGHTS

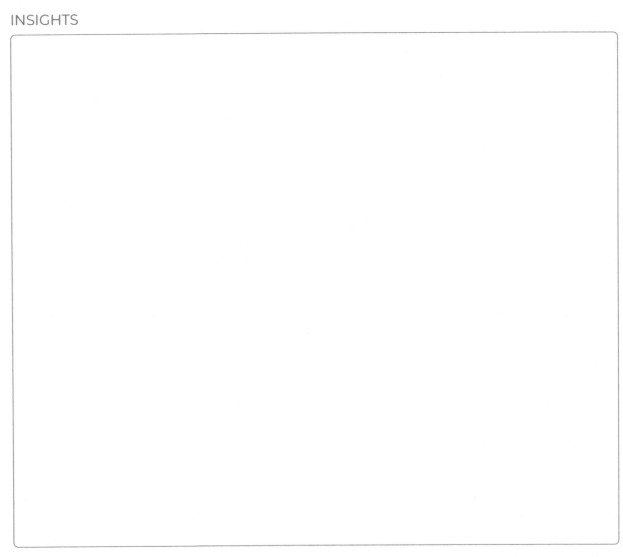

JAN 01 SATURDAY | *Mercury into Aquarius*   CARD OF THE DAY:

▷ INTENTION   ▷ REFLECTION

JAN 02 SUNDAY | ○ *New Moon in Capricorn*   CARD OF THE DAY:

▷ INTENTION   ▷ REFLECTION

JAN 03 MONDAY   CARD OF THE DAY:

▷ INTENTION   ▷ REFLECTION

JAN 04 TUESDAY   CARD OF THE DAY:

▷ INTENTION   ▷ REFLECTION

JAN 05 WEDNESDAY   CARD OF THE DAY:

▷ INTENTION   ▷ REFLECTION

JAN 06 THURSDAY   CARD OF THE DAY:

▷ INTENTION   ▷ REFLECTION

JAN 07 FRIDAY   CARD OF THE DAY:

▷ INTENTION   ▷ REFLECTION

JAN 08 SATURDAY   CARD OF THE DAY:

▷ INTENTION   ▷ REFLECTION

JAN 09 SUNDAY   CARD OF THE DAY:

▷ INTENTION   ▷ REFLECTION

JAN 10 MONDAY   CARD OF THE DAY:

▷ INTENTION   ▷ REFLECTION

JAN 11 TUESDAY   CARD OF THE DAY:

▷ INTENTION   ▷ REFLECTION

JAN 12 WEDNESDAY   CARD OF THE DAY:

▷ INTENTION   ▷ REFLECTION

JAN 13 THURSDAY   CARD OF THE DAY:

▷ INTENTION   ▷ REFLECTION

JAN 14 FRIDAY | *Mercury Retrograde begins*   CARD OF THE DAY:

▷ INTENTION   ▷ REFLECTION

JAN 15 SATURDAY

CARD OF THE DAY:

▷ INTENTION

▷ REFLECTION

JAN 16 SUNDAY

CARD OF THE DAY:

▷ INTENTION

▷ REFLECTION

JAN 17 MONDAY | ● *Full Moon in Cancer*

CARD OF THE DAY:

▷ INTENTION

▷ REFLECTION

JAN 18 TUESDAY

CARD OF THE DAY:

▷ INTENTION

▷ REFLECTION

JAN 19 WEDNESDAY | *Happy Aquarius Season!*

CARD OF THE DAY:

▷ INTENTION

▷ REFLECTION

JAN 20 THURSDAY

CARD OF THE DAY:

▷ INTENTION

▷ REFLECTION

JAN 21 FRIDAY

CARD OF THE DAY:

▷ INTENTION

▷ REFLECTION

JAN 22   SATURDAY   CARD OF THE DAY:

▷ INTENTION   ▷ REFLECTION

JAN 23   SUNDAY   CARD OF THE DAY:

▷ INTENTION   ▷ REFLECTION

JAN 24   MONDAY   CARD OF THE DAY:

▷ INTENTION   ▷ REFLECTION

JAN 25   TUESDAY   CARD OF THE DAY:

▷ INTENTION   ▷ REFLECTION

JAN 26   WEDNESDAY   CARD OF THE DAY:

▷ INTENTION   ▷ REFLECTION

JAN 27   THURSDAY   CARD OF THE DAY:

▷ INTENTION   ▷ REFLECTION

JAN 28   FRIDAY   CARD OF THE DAY:

▷ INTENTION   ▷ REFLECTION

JAN 29 SATURDAY   CARD OF THE DAY:

▷ INTENTION   ▷ REFLECTION

JAN 30 SUNDAY   CARD OF THE DAY:

▷ INTENTION   ▷ REFLECTION

JAN 31 MONDAY | ○ *New Moon in Aquarius*   CARD OF THE DAY:

▷ INTENTION   ▷ REFLECTION

INSIGHTS

FEBRUARY

THE SUN

After the clearing of unhealthy attachments in January, you will emerge with a renewed sense of vitality and radiance with the Sun's influence in February. Tap into your highest potential — your source energy and inner power — by stepping into the light. You are here to make an impact and create positive change in the world. If you are waiting for a sign, this is it! Make the most of this potent, radiant energy. The Sun gives you strength and tells you that no matter where you go or what you do, your positive vibration will radiate, attracting happiness and joy into your life. People are drawn to you, because you can always see the bright side and bring warmth into their lives. This beautiful, warm energy is what will get you through the tough times and help you succeed.

 ### RITUAL: SUNSHINE

When the sun is shining, take a moment to stand outside and soak up its rays. Stand with both feet on the ground, connecting you with the earth. Tilt your face up towards the sun, with your eyes closed. And reach out your arms wide with your fingers spread. With an open heart, receive the energy, vitality and radiance the sun has to offer you. Feel it fill every cell in your body with power and vibrance. You might also like to say an affirmation to yourself as you do this, such as "I am bright, strong, and powerful. I am pure energy."

CRYSTAL: ROSE QUARTZ

This romantic stone is well-known as the ultimate crystal for love and romance. Rose quartz brings peace, kindness, and harmony to our relationships — with others and with ourselves. Rose quartz promotes peace and warmth in romantic relationships, and is also ideal for self-care and acceptance.

ASTROLOGICAL INFLUENCES

February 16 | Venus conjunct Mars: There's a bright spark between Venus and Mars today! All relationships will benefit from the extra "zing". Enjoy the flame — just don't get burned. Consider your long game. Try to balance emotional and physical intimacy.

February 18 | Happy Pisces Season!
Emotion, awareness, fluidity, spirituality, intuition.

February 24 | Mercury square Uranus: Mercury square Uranus may bring unexpected news or inexplicable nervousness. Stay grounded during this time — don't get caught in a mental hyper-flux. Let the shift in perspective spark brilliant new ideas (write them all down!).

INSIGHTS

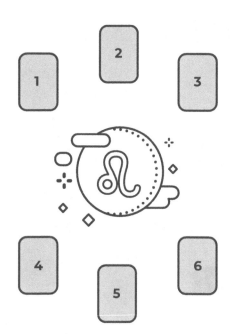

FEBRUARY 16

FULL MOON IN LEO

Feel into the fullness of creativity and play, and get ready to shine with the Leo Full Moon. Celebrate your unique warmth and brilliance bathed in this wonderful energy.

1. What am I most proud of having achieved in the last six months?

2. How has my past courage impacted my personal growth?

3. What are some limiting beliefs I hold about myself?

4. What new stories can I tell myself instead?

5. Where in my life might I need to be more humble?

6. How could I express myself more authentically this year?

INSIGHTS

FEB 01 TUESDAY
CARD OF THE DAY:

▷ INTENTION

▷ REFLECTION

FEB 02 WEDNESDAY
CARD OF THE DAY:

▷ INTENTION

▷ REFLECTION

FEB 03 THURSDAY | *Mercury Retrograde ends*
CARD OF THE DAY:

▷ INTENTION

▷ REFLECTION

FEB 04 FRIDAY
CARD OF THE DAY:

▷ INTENTION

▷ REFLECTION

FEB 05 SATURDAY
CARD OF THE DAY:

▷ INTENTION

▷ REFLECTION

FEB 06 SUNDAY
CARD OF THE DAY:

▷ INTENTION

▷ REFLECTION

FEB 07 MONDAY
CARD OF THE DAY:

▷ INTENTION

▷ REFLECTION

FEB 08 TUESDAY

CARD OF THE DAY:

▷ INTENTION

▷ REFLECTION

FEB 09 WEDNESDAY

CARD OF THE DAY:

▷ INTENTION

▷ REFLECTION

FEB 10 THURSDAY

CARD OF THE DAY:

▷ INTENTION

▷ REFLECTION

FEB 11 FRIDAY

CARD OF THE DAY:

▷ INTENTION

▷ REFLECTION

FEB 12 SATURDAY

CARD OF THE DAY:

▷ INTENTION

▷ REFLECTION

FEB 13 SUNDAY

CARD OF THE DAY:

▷ INTENTION

▷ REFLECTION

FEB 14 MONDAY

CARD OF THE DAY:

▷ INTENTION

▷ REFLECTION

FEB 15   TUESDAY

CARD OF THE DAY:

▷ INTENTION

▷ REFLECTION

FEB 16   WEDNESDAY | ● *Full Moon in Leo*
Venus conjunct Mars

CARD OF THE DAY:

▷ INTENTION

▷ REFLECTION

FEB 17   THURSDAY

CARD OF THE DAY:

▷ INTENTION

▷ REFLECTION

FEB 18   FRIDAY | *Happy Pisces Season!*

CARD OF THE DAY:

▷ INTENTION

▷ REFLECTION

FEB 19   SATURDAY

CARD OF THE DAY:

▷ INTENTION

▷ REFLECTION

FEB 20   SUNDAY

CARD OF THE DAY:

▷ INTENTION

▷ REFLECTION

FEB 21   MONDAY

CARD OF THE DAY:

▷ INTENTION

▷ REFLECTION

FEB 22 TUESDAY

▷ INTENTION

CARD OF THE DAY:

▷ REFLECTION

FEB 23 WEDNESDAY

▷ INTENTION

CARD OF THE DAY:

▷ REFLECTION

FEB 24 THURSDAY | *Mercury square Uranus*

▷ INTENTION

CARD OF THE DAY:

▷ REFLECTION

FEB 25 FRIDAY

▷ INTENTION

CARD OF THE DAY:

▷ REFLECTION

FEB 26 SATURDAY

▷ INTENTION

CARD OF THE DAY:

▷ REFLECTION

FEB 27 SUNDAY

▷ INTENTION

CARD OF THE DAY:

▷ REFLECTION

FEB 28 MONDAY

▷ INTENTION

CARD OF THE DAY:

▷ REFLECTION

MARCH

DEATH

March brings change and transformation, death and rebirth. What must die within you so that a newer, more evolved version of yourself can emerge? As you continue to evolve, you're also rapidly outgrowing yourself — and this is a good thing! There are parts of you (the "old you") that no longer serve your greater vision and are ready to be left in the past — but only if you are willing to let them go. The time has come to shed your skin, let go of the past, and create new ways of being that are much more in alignment with who you truly want to become. Though it may be difficult, the Death card promises renewal and transformation. Remember, if you resist necessary endings, you may experience pain — both emotionally and physically. But if you exercise your imagination and visualize a new possibility, you allow more constructive patterns to emerge.

 ## RITUAL: DEATH AND REBIRTH

This is a powerful ritual, but also very intense — so please do it mindfully. Take out the Death card and light a candle. Meditate on the concept of death and transformation. Then when you are ready, bring your attention inwards and connect with your inner source of energy. Imagine that today is the last day of your life. You are stripped of your past and your identity, and all that is left is your pure source energy. You may even imagine yourself dying, melting into the ground, fading away. Then, imagine yourself being reborn and recreated from that pure source of energy. Experience a sense of peace and deep truth as you step fully into this transformation. You are refreshed and revitalized. And when you are ready, come back into the room and journal your experience.

 ## CRYSTAL: CITRINE

Citrine promotes joy and abundance, making it the perfect stone to balance moodiness and promote gratitude. Citrine is also associated with the throat chakra and communication, and stimulating intellect. Use this powerful stone when gratitude journaling, or for a powerful mood boost!

ASTROLOGICAL INFLUENCES

March 3 | Venus conjunct Pluto: This transit sparks intense longing and transformation. The energy is deep, intense, and highly magnetic. Be careful not to manipulate others into affection or commitment. Vulnerability and trust are paramount.

March 5 | Mars into Aquarius: Social change is amplified. This is a great time to fight for what you believe in! Shelve "the rulebook" for a little while — it's easier to ask for forgiveness than permission, anyway!

March 20 | Happy Aries Season!
Passion, motivation, enthusiasm, assertion, impulsiveness.

INSIGHTS

MARCH 2
NEW MOON IN PISCES

Now is the time to let your imagination run wild and dream big. Tap into your intuition and set intentions to bring your visions to life.

1. How can I connect more deeply with my intuition?

2. What can I do to bring myself into alignment with the highest good?

3. What am I currently manifesting in my life?

4. How can I align my emotions to support positive manifestations?

5. What new creative projects am I called to begin now?

6. How can I further develop my spiritual practice?

INSIGHTS

MARCH 18

FULL MOON IN VIRGO

Honor the ways you are serving the world and the places you are creating order from chaos at this Virgo Full Moon.

1. What can I offer to my family and friends to be of the highest service?

2. Which areas of my life might benefit from creating order?

3. How might I benefit from working hard in the next six months?

4. How can I limit clutter in my physical space?

5. What can I do to better support my mental clarity?

6. How can I best support healthy emotional expression?

INSIGHTS

MARCH 31
NEW MOON IN ARIES

Use the extra dose of Aries courage to set bold intentions at this New Moon. What bold risks would you take if you knew you would succeed?

1. What are the next steps to take to bring myself into alignment with my true desires?

2. Where can I channel my passion to reap rewards in the next six months?

3. What can I become more excited about?

4. How could I be more compassionate toward others?

5. What can I do to bolster my self-confidence?

6. How can I handle conflict more effectively?

INSIGHTS

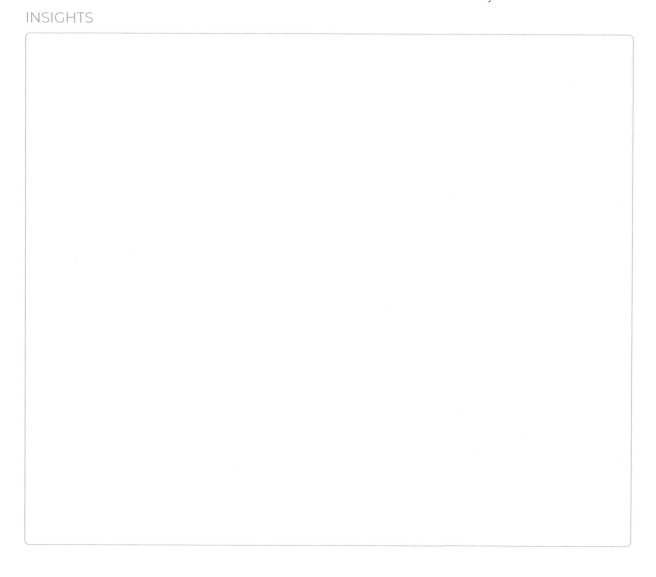

MAR 01 TUESDAY

CARD OF THE DAY:

▷ INTENTION

▷ REFLECTION

MAR 02 WEDNESDAY | ☼ *New Moon in Pisces*

CARD OF THE DAY:

▷ INTENTION

▷ REFLECTION

MAR 03 THURSDAY | *Venus conjunct Pluto*

CARD OF THE DAY:

▷ INTENTION

▷ REFLECTION

MAR 04 FRIDAY

CARD OF THE DAY:

▷ INTENTION

▷ REFLECTION

MAR 05 SATURDAY | *Mars into Aquarius*

CARD OF THE DAY:

▷ INTENTION

▷ REFLECTION

MAR 06 SUNDAY

CARD OF THE DAY:

▷ INTENTION

▷ REFLECTION

MAR 07 MONDAY

CARD OF THE DAY:

▷ INTENTION

▷ REFLECTION

MAR 08 TUESDAY   CARD OF THE DAY:

▷ INTENTION   ▷ REFLECTION

MAR 09 WEDNESDAY   CARD OF THE DAY:

▷ INTENTION   ▷ REFLECTION

MAR 10 THURSDAY   CARD OF THE DAY:

▷ INTENTION   ▷ REFLECTION

MAR 11 FRIDAY   CARD OF THE DAY:

▷ INTENTION   ▷ REFLECTION

MAR 12 SATURDAY   CARD OF THE DAY:

▷ INTENTION   ▷ REFLECTION

MAR 13 SUNDAY   CARD OF THE DAY:

▷ INTENTION   ▷ REFLECTION

MAR 14 MONDAY   CARD OF THE DAY:

▷ INTENTION   ▷ REFLECTION

MAR 15 TUESDAY   CARD OF THE DAY:

▷ INTENTION   ▷ REFLECTION

MAR 16 WEDNESDAY   CARD OF THE DAY:

▷ INTENTION   ▷ REFLECTION

MAR 17 THURSDAY   CARD OF THE DAY:

▷ INTENTION   ▷ REFLECTION

MAR 18 FRIDAY | ● Full Moon in Virgo   CARD OF THE DAY:

▷ INTENTION   ▷ REFLECTION

MAR 19 SATURDAY   CARD OF THE DAY:

▷ INTENTION   ▷ REFLECTION

MAR 20 SUNDAY | Happy Aries Season!   CARD OF THE DAY:

▷ INTENTION   ▷ REFLECTION

MAR 21 MONDAY   CARD OF THE DAY:

▷ INTENTION   ▷ REFLECTION

MAR 22 TUESDAY

CARD OF THE DAY:

▷ INTENTION

▷ REFLECTION

MAR 23 WEDNESDAY

CARD OF THE DAY:

▷ INTENTION

▷ REFLECTION

MAR 24 THURSDAY

CARD OF THE DAY:

▷ INTENTION

▷ REFLECTION

MAR 25 FRIDAY

CARD OF THE DAY:

▷ INTENTION

▷ REFLECTION

MAR 26 SATURDAY

CARD OF THE DAY:

▷ INTENTION

▷ REFLECTION

MAR 27 SUNDAY

CARD OF THE DAY:

▷ INTENTION

▷ REFLECTION

MAR 28 MONDAY

CARD OF THE DAY:

▷ INTENTION

▷ REFLECTION

MAR 29 TUESDAY
CARD OF THE DAY:

▷ INTENTION

▷ REFLECTION

MAR 30 WEDNESDAY
CARD OF THE DAY:

▷ INTENTION

▷ REFLECTION

MAR 31 THURSDAY | ○ *New Moon in Aries*
CARD OF THE DAY:

▷ INTENTION

▷ REFLECTION

INSIGHTS

SPRING EQUINOX SPREAD

The Spring Equinox (March 20, 8:33 a.m. PT; September 23, 11:03 a.m. AEST) honors new growth and opportunity. The seeds have been planted and nurtured by the rain, now they are emerging from the earth into the brightness of the sunlight, blossoming into beautiful flowers, fruit, and foliage. Springtime is filled with color, scents, and a feeling of excitement and anticipation of what's to come. It's the perfect time to explore new possibilities, start new projects, and truly bloom under the rays of this positive light.

Use the following Tarot spread around the time of the Spring Equinox to connect with this sacred energy.

1. What has emerged for me over the Winter period?

2. What lessons have I learned?

3. What new seeds are beginning to sprout?

4. How can I nurture these new opportunities?

5. How am I truly blossoming?

6. How can I best embrace the Spring energy?

INSIGHTS

INSIGHTS

SPRING EQUINOX INTENTIONS

Holding the energy and insight of your Spring Equinox Tarot Reading, set your intentions for the next three months:

APRIL

THE HERMIT

This month you may feel called to retreat from everyday life and embark on a spiritual journey, as The Hermit invites you to bring deep awareness to your life. Draw your energy inward and find the answers you seek, deep within your soul. Soon, you will come to realize that your most profound sense of truth is within you, and not in the distractions of the outside world. April is the perfect time to go on a weekend retreat or sacred pilgrimage, anything in which you can contemplate your motivations, personal values and principles, and get closer to your authentic self. If you're at a pivotal point in your life and considering a new direction, use meditation and self-examination to re-evaluate your personal goals and change your overall course.

 ## RITUAL: SPIRITUAL RETREAT

Choose a day (or weekend, week, or even month) where you can retreat from your everyday life and experience a period of solitude and reflection. Disconnect from technology, go on a hike, travel to a remote location, book an AirBnB, or even schedule a staycation at home — just make sure it's somewhere you won't be disturbed and where you can have an extended period on your own. Take along your journal, Tarot and oracle cards, and spend time simply reflecting on your life and what you have learned along the way. Honor the stillness from within, and reconnect with your inner guiding light to show you the way forward.

 ## CRYSTAL: CARNELIAN

Carnelian is a stabilizing stone, providing motivation and grounding. Carnelian balances the root chakra and promotes courage and wise decision-making. Allow Carnelian to guide you in trusting yourself to make the best choices for you, and overcome any limiting beliefs that keep you at a standstill.

 ## ASTROLOGICAL INFLUENCES

April 12 | Jupiter conjunct Neptune: Space for spiritual and self-development. It's the perfect time to reconnect with your favorite Tarot decks, or spend some extra time journaling or meditating.

April 19 | Happy Taurus Season!
Stability, reliability, affection, sensuality, indulgence.

April 29 | Mercury into Gemini: Mercury flies into Gemini today, strengthening communication. It's a great time to learn — enroll in a short course, or teach others how to do something you're great at. Connect with friends and fill up your social calendar!

INSIGHTS

APRIL 16

FULL MOON IN LIBRA

The Libra Full Moon invites you to revel in beauty and release the things that negatively impact your sense of harmony and balance.

1. What support might I benefit from to help me make the best choices?

2. What can I do to create more balance in my closest relationships?

3. Where is the greatest imbalance in my life right now?

4. What do I need to release in order to be more objective moving forward?

5. What do I need to do to feel more steadfast in my decision-making?

6. How can I manifest more beauty in my life?

INSIGHTS

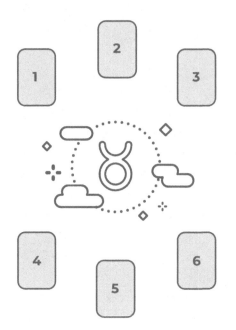

APRIL 30 | SOLAR ECLIPSE

NEW MOON IN TAURUS

With the New Moon in Taurus, you have the chance to become conscious about creating peaceful and pleasurable experiences in your life. Use this energy to develop empowering new habits.

1. What can I do to inspire tranquility in my home?

2. What lessons can I learn from nature?

3. How can I release unhealthy attachments to physical possessions?

4. What simple pleasures would I most enjoy right now?

5. What activities will help me become more grounded in my physical self?

6. What can I do to manage overindulgence?

INSIGHTS

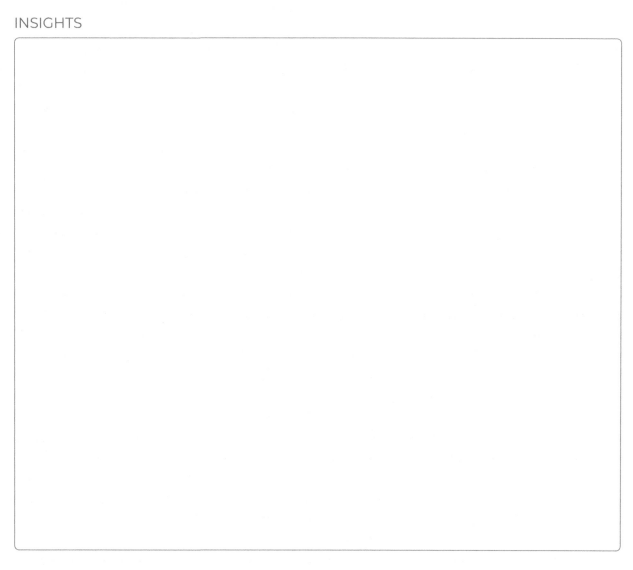

APR 01   FRIDAY   CARD OF THE DAY:

▷ INTENTION   ▷ REFLECTION

APR 02   SATURDAY   CARD OF THE DAY:

▷ INTENTION   ▷ REFLECTION

APR 03   SUNDAY   CARD OF THE DAY:

▷ INTENTION   ▷ REFLECTION

APR 04   MONDAY   CARD OF THE DAY:

▷ INTENTION   ▷ REFLECTION

APR 05   TUESDAY   CARD OF THE DAY:

▷ INTENTION   ▷ REFLECTION

APR 06   WEDNESDAY   CARD OF THE DAY:

▷ INTENTION   ▷ REFLECTION

APR 07   THURSDAY   CARD OF THE DAY:

▷ INTENTION   ▷ REFLECTION

APR 08   FRIDAY

CARD OF THE DAY:

▷ INTENTION

▷ REFLECTION

APR 09   SATURDAY

CARD OF THE DAY:

▷ INTENTION

▷ REFLECTION

APR 10   SUNDAY

CARD OF THE DAY:

▷ INTENTION

▷ REFLECTION

APR 11   MONDAY

CARD OF THE DAY:

▷ INTENTION

▷ REFLECTION

APR 12   TUESDAY | *Jupiter conjunct Neptune*

CARD OF THE DAY:

▷ INTENTION

▷ REFLECTION

APR 13   WEDNESDAY

CARD OF THE DAY:

▷ INTENTION

▷ REFLECTION

APR 14   THURSDAY

CARD OF THE DAY:

▷ INTENTION

▷ REFLECTION

APR 15   FRIDAY

▷ INTENTION   ▷ REFLECTION

CARD OF THE DAY:

APR 16   SATURDAY | ● *Full Moon in Libra*

▷ INTENTION   ▷ REFLECTION

CARD OF THE DAY:

APR 17   SUNDAY

▷ INTENTION   ▷ REFLECTION

CARD OF THE DAY:

APR 18   MONDAY

▷ INTENTION   ▷ REFLECTION

CARD OF THE DAY:

APR 19   TUESDAY | *Happy Taurus Season!*

▷ INTENTION   ▷ REFLECTION

CARD OF THE DAY:

APR 20   WEDNESDAY

▷ INTENTION   ▷ REFLECTION

CARD OF THE DAY:

APR 21   THURSDAY

▷ INTENTION   ▷ REFLECTION

CARD OF THE DAY:

APR 22 FRIDAY

CARD OF THE DAY:

▷ INTENTION

▷ REFLECTION

APR 23 SATURDAY

CARD OF THE DAY:

▷ INTENTION

▷ REFLECTION

APR 24 SUNDAY

CARD OF THE DAY:

▷ INTENTION

▷ REFLECTION

APR 25 MONDAY

CARD OF THE DAY:

▷ INTENTION

▷ REFLECTION

APR 26 TUESDAY

CARD OF THE DAY:

▷ INTENTION

▷ REFLECTION

APR 27 WEDNESDAY

CARD OF THE DAY:

▷ INTENTION

▷ REFLECTION

APR 28 THURSDAY

CARD OF THE DAY:

▷ INTENTION

▷ REFLECTION

APR 29   FRIDAY | *Mercury into Gemini*   CARD OF THE DAY:

▷ INTENTION

▷ REFLECTION

APR 30   SATURDAY | ☼ *New Moon in Taurus*   CARD OF THE DAY:

▷ INTENTION

▷ REFLECTION

INSIGHTS

MAY

THE WORLD

May brings a sense of wholeness and completion as all your triumphs and tribulations come full circle. Everything you have experienced, good and bad, has led you to this moment. You are in the right place, doing the right thing, and achieving what you have envisioned. You feel whole and complete. You also have a deep appreciation for your achievements and spiritual lessons learned. Express gratitude for what you have created and received. It's also a good time to tie up any loose ends so you're ready to embrace any new opportunities flowing your way.

 ### RITUAL: GRATITUDE AND CLOSURE

Take out The World card from your Tarot deck and place it in front of you. Light a candle and say out loud, "I open this sacred space and give thanks for all that I have experienced." Now, reflect on your achievements, opportunities, and challenges of the past month and the past year, and write them down in your journal. Now, reflect on what you have learned and write these lessons down. Finally, reflect on how you can bring a sense of closure and completion to this cycle. To end the ritual, blow out the candle, saying out loud, "I close this sacred space and give thanks for all that I have experienced."

CRYSTAL: PYRITE

A stone of protection and purity, it's the perfect crystal to guard against energy vampires. It shields us from energetic attacks, and allows us to cut through negative vibrations. A powerful stone for silencing the mind's negative thoughts, allowing us to focus on what is good and pure in the world.

ASTROLOGICAL INFLUENCES

May 10–June 3 | Mercury Retrograde: Utilize the Tarot Reader's Survival Guide for Mercury Retrograde inside of your Toolkit at www.biddytarot.com/2022-planner-bonus to help navigate through this time.

May 20 | Happy Gemini Season!
Communication, logic, enthusiasm, light-heartedness, adaptability.

May 22 | Mercury into Taurus: Taurus brings a down-to-earth, stable element to Mercury. Common sense will serve you well. "If it ain't broken, don't fix it" will save you headaches — but don't slip into a rigid frame of mind.

INSIGHTS

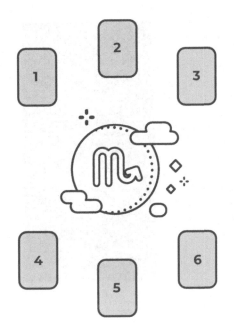

MAY 15 | LUNAR ECLIPSE
FULL MOON IN SCORPIO

Intense energies surround the Scorpio Full Moon, creating an ideal time for shadow work and transformational activities. Use this energy to release anything that no longer resonates with your true self.

1. What feelings have I been avoiding?

2. What lessons have I learned through trying times in the past six months?

3. What intense emotions are coming up for me now?

4. How can I express my emotions more healthily?

5. What do I need to release in order to experience deep transformation?

6. Where do I need to relinquish control in my life?

INSIGHTS

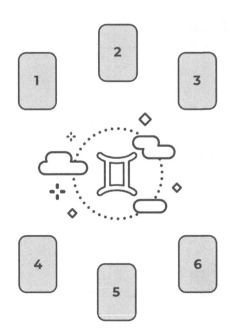

MAY 30

NEW MOON IN GEMINI

A fresh New Moon in Gemini brings a sense of lightness. Set intentions around what you want to learn and teach, and how you can communicate for maximum effect.

1. How can I enhance my perceptions of the world around me?

2. What am I most curious about right now?

3. Where do I need to learn to verbalize my emotions?

4. What do I have to teach others?

5. What lessons can I learn from others?

6. How can I communicate with others in new and innovative ways?

INSIGHTS

Don't forget to snap a pic of your reading and share on IG using the hashtag **#biddytarotplanner**.
We love seeing you using your Biddy Tarot Planner in action and can't wait to celebrate with you!

MAY | 61

MAY 01 SUNDAY
CARD OF THE DAY:

▷ INTENTION

▷ REFLECTION

MAY 02 MONDAY
CARD OF THE DAY:

▷ INTENTION

▷ REFLECTION

MAY 03 TUESDAY
CARD OF THE DAY:

▷ INTENTION

▷ REFLECTION

MAY 04 WEDNESDAY
CARD OF THE DAY:

▷ INTENTION

▷ REFLECTION

MAY 05 THURSDAY
CARD OF THE DAY:

▷ INTENTION

▷ REFLECTION

MAY 06 FRIDAY
CARD OF THE DAY:

▷ INTENTION

▷ REFLECTION

MAY 07 SATURDAY
CARD OF THE DAY:

▷ INTENTION

▷ REFLECTION

MAY 08 SUNDAY

CARD OF THE DAY:

▷ INTENTION

▷ REFLECTION

MAY 09 MONDAY

CARD OF THE DAY:

▷ INTENTION

▷ REFLECTION

MAY 10 TUESDAY | *Mercury Retrograde Begins*

CARD OF THE DAY:

▷ INTENTION

▷ REFLECTION

MAY 11 WEDNESDAY

CARD OF THE DAY:

▷ INTENTION

▷ REFLECTION

MAY 12 THURSDAY

CARD OF THE DAY:

▷ INTENTION

▷ REFLECTION

MAY 13 FRIDAY

CARD OF THE DAY:

▷ INTENTION

▷ REFLECTION

MAY 14 SATURDAY

CARD OF THE DAY:

▷ INTENTION

▷ REFLECTION

MAY 15   SUNDAY | ● *Full Moon in Scorpio*   CARD OF THE DAY:

▷ INTENTION   ▷ REFLECTION

MAY 16   MONDAY   CARD OF THE DAY:

▷ INTENTION   ▷ REFLECTION

MAY 17   TUESDAY   CARD OF THE DAY:

▷ INTENTION   ▷ REFLECTION

MAY 18   WEDNESDAY   CARD OF THE DAY:

▷ INTENTION   ▷ REFLECTION

MAY 19   THURSDAY   CARD OF THE DAY:

▷ INTENTION   ▷ REFLECTION

MAY 20   FRIDAY | *Happy Gemini Season!*   CARD OF THE DAY:

▷ INTENTION   ▷ REFLECTION

MAY 21   SATURDAY   CARD OF THE DAY:

▷ INTENTION   ▷ REFLECTION

MAY 22 SUNDAY | *Mercury into Taurus*   CARD OF THE DAY:

▷ INTENTION   ▷ REFLECTION

MAY 23 MONDAY   CARD OF THE DAY:

▷ INTENTION   ▷ REFLECTION

MAY 24 TUESDAY   CARD OF THE DAY:

▷ INTENTION   ▷ REFLECTION

MAY 25 WEDNESDAY   CARD OF THE DAY:

▷ INTENTION   ▷ REFLECTION

MAY 26 THURSDAY   CARD OF THE DAY:

▷ INTENTION   ▷ REFLECTION

MAY 27 FRIDAY   CARD OF THE DAY:

▷ INTENTION   ▷ REFLECTION

MAY 28 SATURDAY   CARD OF THE DAY:

▷ INTENTION   ▷ REFLECTION

MAY 29   SUNDAY   CARD OF THE DAY:

▷ INTENTION   ▷ REFLECTION

MAY 30   MONDAY | ○ New Moon in Gemini   CARD OF THE DAY:

▷ INTENTION   ▷ REFLECTION

MAY 31   TUESDAY   CARD OF THE DAY:

▷ INTENTION   ▷ REFLECTION

INSIGHTS

JUNE

TEMPERANCE

Temperance invites you to create balance and harmony in your life. Look at where you have invested your energy over the past few months, especially when it comes to work, relationships, and self-care. Where have you invested too much or too little energy? Is this in alignment with your vision and your goals? While you may feel regret about where you have over- or under-invested your time and energy, be kind to yourself. Know that it's impossible to create perfect balance in every moment. The key is in making conscious decisions about where you invest your time and energy, and creating balance *over time* that is aligned with your highest vision. Harmonize your various passions, interests, and goals so that you can move forward with a sense of wholeness and completion.

 RITUAL: BALANCING YOUR ENERGY AND FLOW

Pull out the Temperance card from your favorite deck, and place it nearby as your guide throughout this ritual. On a piece of paper, draw a line down the middle. On the left, write down all the areas of your life that you have poured your energy into recently. Acknowledge all the positive outcomes you have experienced as a result of dedicating your energy to these areas. Then on the right, write down all the areas you have neglected recently. Make a commitment to re-engage with these areas this month and give them some love.

 CRYSTAL: CHRYSOPRASE

Chrysoprase is a beautiful, gentle stone which opens the heart and warms the spirit. Also known as the Stone of Venus, Chrysoprase symbolizes happiness, good fortune and abundance. Allow Chrysoprase to help you see the unique beauty within yourself, allowing your true self to shine with courage and grace.

 ASTROLOGICAL INFLUENCES

June 18 | Venus square Saturn: Saturn brings a coolness to romantic Venus. Use this time for self-care — especially if your confidence is low. Don't read into things too much; instead, engage in self-reflection. Financial stress may heighten feelings of anxiety.

June 21 | Happy Cancer Season!
Nurturing, emotional, protective, romantic, loyal.

June 22 | Venus into Gemini: During this transit, variety (and witty repartee!) is the spice of life. Loosen up, have fun, and don't take love so seriously. Lean into light communication with others, bonding on a mental level.

INSIGHTS

JUNE 14

FULL MOON IN SAGITTARIUS

Ideals and visions are heightened with this Full Moon in Sagittarius. Tap into this expansive energy and release anything that is keeping you small.

1. Where do I need to focus on expanding my awareness?

2. What do I need to release in order to achieve my goals?

3. What is my ideal vision for the global community?

4. How might short- or long-term travel benefit me in the next six months?

5. What can I do to connect more deeply with my friends?

6. What do I need to let go of in order to truly inspire others?

INSIGHTS

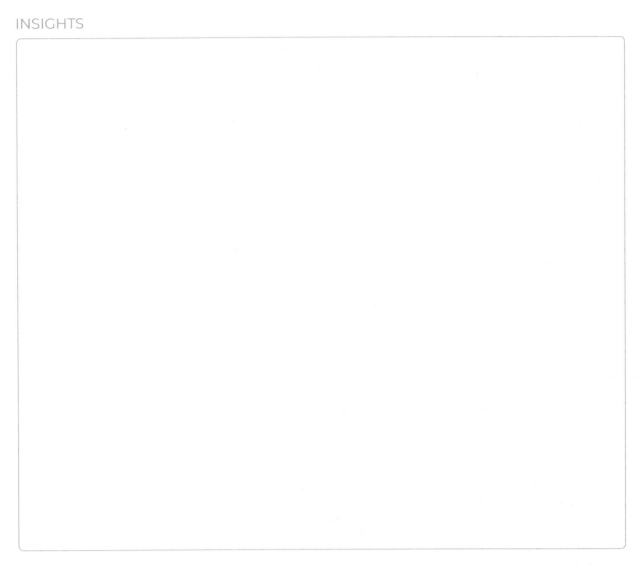

NEW MOON
IN CANCER

If there were ever a time to make conscious choices about how you feel day-to-day, the New Moon in Cancer is the time. Dive into your emotional world and set empowering intentions around how you want to feel.

1. What new feelings are coming up for me right now?

2. Where do I need to empower myself to be more vulnerable in my relationships?

3. How might I benefit from setting boundaries?

4. How can I level-up my self-care practice?

5. What do I need to know about creating sacred space in my home?

6. What new approach can I take to support my emotional well-being?

INSIGHTS

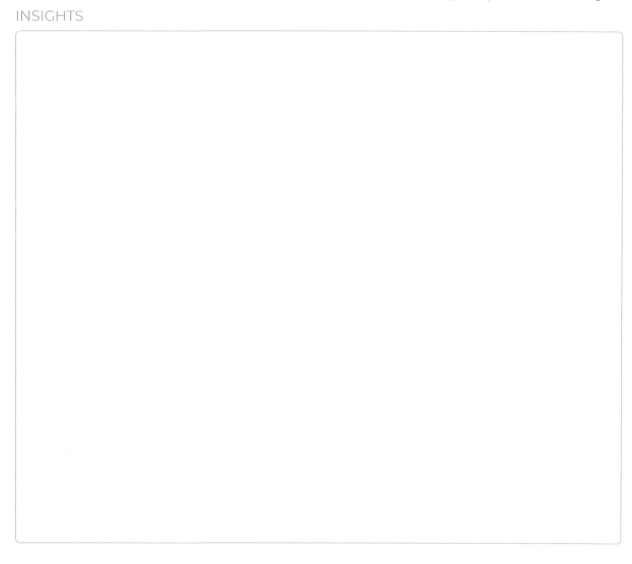

JUN 01   WEDNESDAY   CARD OF THE DAY:

▷ INTENTION   ▷ REFLECTION

JUN 02   THURSDAY   CARD OF THE DAY:

▷ INTENTION   ▷ REFLECTION

JUN 03   FRIDAY | *Mercury Retrograde ends*   CARD OF THE DAY:

▷ INTENTION   ▷ REFLECTION

JUN 04   SATURDAY   CARD OF THE DAY:

▷ INTENTION   ▷ REFLECTION

JUN 05   SUNDAY   CARD OF THE DAY:

▷ INTENTION   ▷ REFLECTION

JUN 06   MONDAY   CARD OF THE DAY:

▷ INTENTION   ▷ REFLECTION

JUN 07   TUESDAY   CARD OF THE DAY:

▷ INTENTION   ▷ REFLECTION

JUN 08 WEDNESDAY   CARD OF THE DAY:

▷ INTENTION   ▷ REFLECTION

JUN 09 THURSDAY   CARD OF THE DAY:

▷ INTENTION   ▷ REFLECTION

JUN 10 FRIDAY   CARD OF THE DAY:

▷ INTENTION   ▷ REFLECTION

JUN 11 SATURDAY   CARD OF THE DAY:

▷ INTENTION   ▷ REFLECTION

JUN 12 SUNDAY   CARD OF THE DAY:

▷ INTENTION   ▷ REFLECTION

JUN 13 MONDAY   CARD OF THE DAY:

▷ INTENTION   ▷ REFLECTION

JUN 14 TUESDAY | ● *Full Moon in Sagittarius*   CARD OF THE DAY:

▷ INTENTION   ▷ REFLECTION

JUN 15   WEDNESDAY   CARD OF THE DAY:

▷ INTENTION   ▷ REFLECTION

JUN 16   THURSDAY   CARD OF THE DAY:

▷ INTENTION   ▷ REFLECTION

JUN 17   FRIDAY   CARD OF THE DAY:

▷ INTENTION   ▷ REFLECTION

JUN 18   SATURDAY | *Venus square Saturn*   CARD OF THE DAY:

▷ INTENTION   ▷ REFLECTION

JUN 19   SUNDAY   CARD OF THE DAY:

▷ INTENTION   ▷ REFLECTION

JUN 20   MONDAY   CARD OF THE DAY:

▷ INTENTION   ▷ REFLECTION

JUN 21   TUESDAY | *Happy Cancer Season!*   CARD OF THE DAY:

▷ INTENTION   ▷ REFLECTION

JUN 22 WEDNESDAY | *Venus into Gemini*   CARD OF THE DAY:

▷ INTENTION   ▷ REFLECTION

JUN 23 THURSDAY   CARD OF THE DAY:

▷ INTENTION   ▷ REFLECTION

JUN 24 FRIDAY   CARD OF THE DAY:

▷ INTENTION   ▷ REFLECTION

JUN 25 SATURDAY   CARD OF THE DAY:

▷ INTENTION   ▷ REFLECTION

JUN 26 SUNDAY   CARD OF THE DAY:

▷ INTENTION   ▷ REFLECTION

JUN 27 MONDAY   CARD OF THE DAY:

▷ INTENTION   ▷ REFLECTION

JUN 28 TUESDAY | ◌ *New Moon in Cancer*   CARD OF THE DAY:

▷ INTENTION   ▷ REFLECTION

JUN 29 WEDNESDAY   CARD OF THE DAY:

▷ INTENTION   ▷ REFLECTION

JUN 30 THURSDAY   CARD OF THE DAY:

▷ INTENTION   ▷ REFLECTION

INSIGHTS

SUMMER SOLSTICE SPREAD

The Summer Solstice (June 21, 2:13 a.m. PT; December 22, 8:48 a.m. AEST) is the time to shine and be seen! Be ready to step into the spotlight and express your true self to the world. Bask in the sunrays and allow yourself to be filled with light as you revel in a sense of accomplishment and fulfilment. Now's the time! Watch as your projects crest towards completion and you are energized to take action on the new opportunities that arose during the Springtime.

Use the following Tarot spread around the time of the Summer Solstice to connect with this sacred energy.

1. What new opportunities have emerged over the Spring?

2. How can I bring my current projects to fruition?

3. What is expanding in my life right now?

4. What blessings am I receiving?

5. What truly fulfills me?

6. How can I shine my light in the world?

INSIGHTS

INSIGHTS

SUMMER SOLSTICE INTENTIONS

Holding the energy and insight of your Summer Solstice Tarot Reading, set your intentions for the next three months:

JULY

THE MAGICIAN

It's time to activate your manifestation superpowers, my friend! With The Magician in July, you have everything you need to make your dreams a reality. Connect with your vision, gather your tools and resources, and start putting your ideas into action. Now is the perfect time to move forward on an idea that you recently conceived. The seed of potential has sprouted, and you are being called to take action and bring your intention to fruition. The skills, knowledge, and capabilities you have gathered along your life path have led you to where you are now, and whether or not you know it, you are ready to turn your ideas into reality.

RITUAL: MANIFEST YOUR VISION

Pull out The Magician from your favorite Tarot deck and place the card nearby to serve as your guide throughout this ritual. On a piece of paper, write down your vision for a new idea that has been on your mind. What is it that you want to bring into fruition? Then, brainstorm all of the tools and resources that you already have available to you and how you can use them to bring your dream to life. Finally, close your eyes and visualize your goal. See everything falling into place, easily and effortlessly, to achieve your dream. Then, when you're ready, open your eyes and say out loud, "So be it!"

⚘ CRYSTAL: SMOKY QUARTZ

Smoky Quartz helps to absorb negative energy and supports positive mental health. It's the perfect stone to use during a Tarot reading to protect against negative energy, and aid in grounding and cord-cutting. Be sure to regularly cleanse and charge Smoky Quartz with your favorite herb bundle, or by the light of the Full Moon.

🪐 ASTROLOGICAL INFLUENCES

July 1 | Mars square Pluto: You may feel a lack of control while Mars squares Pluto, or as though nothing can satisfy you. Be mindful not to bully others while trying to get what you want. Now is the time for strategy, not action.

July 19 | Mercury into Leo: Mercury in Leo brings confidence in self-expression! Contemplate big goals without getting lost in little details. Speak from the heart and stand your ground. Hold space for others to share their own big dreams, too.

July 22 | Happy Leo Season!
Pride, courage, warmth, audacity, generosity.

INSIGHTS

JULY 13

FULL MOON IN CAPRICORN

The Full Moon in Capricorn is a powerful time to reflect on your achievements. Where have you stood in integrity and built something you're proud of?

1. What am I most proud of achieving in the past six months?

2. What foundations do I most need to establish now to support future success?

3. What is a non-negotiable for me right now?

4. How can I help motivate others to work toward their own goals?

5. Which limiting beliefs are preventing me from setting bigger goals?

6. Where do I need to make more ethical choices?

INSIGHTS

JULY 28

NEW MOON
IN LEO

Your creations and passions are coming into focus with the New Moon in Leo. A time for setting courageous intentions about how you want to show up in the world.

1. What do I most want to create?

2. What can I do to express myself authentically in healthy, empowered ways?

3. What new aspects of myself am I discovering?

4. How can I be an effective and compassionate leader?

5. Where am I best placed to lead by example?

6. Which areas of my life may require more courage in the next six months?

INSIGHTS

JUL 01   FRIDAY | *Mars square Pluto*   CARD OF THE DAY:

▷ INTENTION   ▷ REFLECTION

JUL 02   SATURDAY   CARD OF THE DAY:

▷ INTENTION   ▷ REFLECTION

JUL 03   SUNDAY   CARD OF THE DAY:

▷ INTENTION   ▷ REFLECTION

JUL 04   MONDAY   CARD OF THE DAY:

▷ INTENTION   ▷ REFLECTION

JUL 05   TUESDAY   CARD OF THE DAY:

▷ INTENTION   ▷ REFLECTION

JUL 06   WEDNESDAY   CARD OF THE DAY:

▷ INTENTION   ▷ REFLECTION

JUL 07   THURSDAY   CARD OF THE DAY:

▷ INTENTION   ▷ REFLECTION

JUL 08 FRIDAY

CARD OF THE DAY:

▷ INTENTION

▷ REFLECTION

JUL 09 SATURDAY

CARD OF THE DAY:

▷ INTENTION

▷ REFLECTION

JUL 10 SUNDAY

CARD OF THE DAY:

▷ INTENTION

▷ REFLECTION

JUL 11 MONDAY

CARD OF THE DAY:

▷ INTENTION

▷ REFLECTION

JUL 12 TUESDAY

CARD OF THE DAY:

▷ INTENTION

▷ REFLECTION

JUL 13 WEDNESDAY | ● *Full Moon in Capricorn*

CARD OF THE DAY:

▷ INTENTION

▷ REFLECTION

JUL 14 THURSDAY

CARD OF THE DAY:

▷ INTENTION

▷ REFLECTION

JUL 15   FRIDAY

CARD OF THE DAY:

▷ INTENTION

▷ REFLECTION

JUL 16   SATURDAY

CARD OF THE DAY:

▷ INTENTION

▷ REFLECTION

JUL 17   SUNDAY

CARD OF THE DAY:

▷ INTENTION

▷ REFLECTION

JUL 18   MONDAY

CARD OF THE DAY:

▷ INTENTION

▷ REFLECTION

JUL 19   TUESDAY | *Mercury into Leo*

CARD OF THE DAY:

▷ INTENTION

▷ REFLECTION

JUL 20   WEDNESDAY

CARD OF THE DAY:

▷ INTENTION

▷ REFLECTION

JUL 21   THURSDAY

CARD OF THE DAY:

▷ INTENTION

▷ REFLECTION

JUL 22   FRIDAY | *Happy Leo Season!*   CARD OF THE DAY:

▷ INTENTION   ▷ REFLECTION

JUL 23   SATURDAY   CARD OF THE DAY:

▷ INTENTION   ▷ REFLECTION

JUL 24   SUNDAY   CARD OF THE DAY:

▷ INTENTION   ▷ REFLECTION

JUL 25   MONDAY   CARD OF THE DAY:

▷ INTENTION   ▷ REFLECTION

JUL 26   TUESDAY   CARD OF THE DAY:

▷ INTENTION   ▷ REFLECTION

JUL 27   WEDNESDAY   CARD OF THE DAY:

▷ INTENTION   ▷ REFLECTION

JUL 28   THURSDAY | ☼ *New Moon in Leo*   CARD OF THE DAY:

▷ INTENTION   ▷ REFLECTION

JUL 29 FRIDAY   CARD OF THE DAY:

▷ INTENTION   ▷ REFLECTION

JUL 30 SATURDAY   CARD OF THE DAY:

▷ INTENTION   ▷ REFLECTION

JUL 31 SUNDAY   CARD OF THE DAY:

▷ INTENTION   ▷ REFLECTION

INSIGHTS

AUGUST

WHEEL OF FORTUNE

Having put the wheels in motion with The Magician last month, success and good fortune are coming to you — if you are open to receiving it. The Wheel of Fortune reminds you to be optimistic and have faith that the Universe will take care of your situation in the best way possible. Keep your mind open to all kinds of synchronicities and signs from the Universe that will help to guide you along the way, and continue to align your energy and actions with your vision to bring increased abundance and prosperity to you. However, be aware that change is inevitable and while you are experiencing success right now, it may not always be the way. The Wheel of Fortune is a reminder that everything in life occurs within a cycle. Cherish the blissful moments in your life and make the most of them while they are within reach — because in a flash they could be gone.

 ### RITUAL: GRATITUDE FOR GOOD FORTUNE

Find the Wheel of Fortune card from your favorite deck and place it in front of you. Take a moment to look at the image and draw in the energy of this card. Then, in your journal, note down all the areas in your life where you are experiencing good fortune and luck right now. As you do this, feel every cell within your body fill with the golden light of success and abundance. Read through your list and as you do, give thanks to the Universe for supporting your success.

 ### CRYSTAL: TIGER EYE

Use Tiger Eye to ramp up joy, courage, and authenticity. Tiger Eye is used to promote inner strength, confidence, and good luck, and helps to combat feelings of anxiousness or weariness. It's a beautiful stone to incorporate into Tarot readings centered around joy and gratitude, or to carry with you after a challenging reading.

 ### ASTROLOGICAL INFLUENCES

August 11 | Venus into Leo: This "go big or go home" energy brings grandeur to love! This is a time for sweep-them-off-their-feet moments, and validating each other's needs and desires. Express adoration for the people you love — from the heart.

August 16 | Mercury trine Uranus: Communications get a "zap" today — you'll be receptive to new and interesting ideas. Connect with a variety of people and different perspectives. Focus on all things technology.

August 22 | Happy Virgo Season!
Practicality, order, creativity, analysis, service.

INSIGHTS

AUGUST 11
FULL MOON IN AQUARIUS

This Full Moon in Aquarius amplifies the energy of the water bearer, bringing it into laser-sharp focus. Consider the impact your day-to-day choices may be having on a much wider, even global, scale.

1. How can I utilize my unique gifts to contribute to global change?

2. Which beliefs may be having a detrimental affect on my community?

3. What global causes can I champion to have a greater impact on the world?

4. How can I help others to examine their beliefs about the global community?

5. Which forms of communication might I need to limit or release?

6. What can I do to empower others to become more vulnerable?

INSIGHTS

On Instagram? Post a photo of your spread and your Tarot Planner with the hashtag **#biddytarotplanner** and we'll share with the Biddy Tarot community!

86 | 2022 BIDDY TAROT PLANNER

AUGUST 27

NEW MOON IN VIRGO

The New Moon in Virgo is an opportunity to get clear on how you want to be of service in the world and set your intentions around stepping into mastery. What will the best version of yourself be focused on during this lunar cycle?

1. How can I be of the highest service to my family, friends, and partner?

2. Which area of my life would benefit most from evaluating my routine?

3. What change can I make to support my physical health and wellbeing?

4. What action can I take to bring a sense of order to my home?

5. What action can I take to process my thoughts more effectively?

6. What action can I take to gain further emotional clarity?

INSIGHTS

AUG 01 MONDAY   CARD OF THE DAY:

▷ INTENTION   ▷ REFLECTION

AUG 02 TUESDAY   CARD OF THE DAY:

▷ INTENTION   ▷ REFLECTION

AUG 03 WEDNESDAY   CARD OF THE DAY:

▷ INTENTION   ▷ REFLECTION

AUG 04 THURSDAY   CARD OF THE DAY:

▷ INTENTION   ▷ REFLECTION

AUG 05 FRIDAY   CARD OF THE DAY:

▷ INTENTION   ▷ REFLECTION

AUG 06 SATURDAY   CARD OF THE DAY:

▷ INTENTION   ▷ REFLECTION

AUG 07 SUNDAY   CARD OF THE DAY:

▷ INTENTION   ▷ REFLECTION

AUG 08 MONDAY   CARD OF THE DAY:

▷ INTENTION   ▷ REFLECTION

AUG 09 TUESDAY   CARD OF THE DAY:

▷ INTENTION   ▷ REFLECTION

AUG 10 WEDNESDAY   CARD OF THE DAY:

▷ INTENTION   ▷ REFLECTION

AUG 11 THURSDAY | ● *Full Moon in Aquarius*   CARD OF THE DAY:
                         Venus into Leo

▷ INTENTION   ▷ REFLECTION

AUG 12 FRIDAY   CARD OF THE DAY:

▷ INTENTION   ▷ REFLECTION

AUG 13 SATURDAY   CARD OF THE DAY:

▷ INTENTION   ▷ REFLECTION

AUG 14 SUNDAY   CARD OF THE DAY:

▷ INTENTION   ▷ REFLECTION

AUG 15   MONDAY

CARD OF THE DAY:

▷ INTENTION

▷ REFLECTION

AUG 16   TUESDAY | *Mercury trine Uranus*

CARD OF THE DAY:

▷ INTENTION

▷ REFLECTION

AUG 17   WEDNESDAY

CARD OF THE DAY:

▷ INTENTION

▷ REFLECTION

AUG 18   THURSDAY

CARD OF THE DAY:

▷ INTENTION

▷ REFLECTION

AUG 19   FRIDAY

CARD OF THE DAY:

▷ INTENTION

▷ REFLECTION

AUG 20   SATURDAY

CARD OF THE DAY:

▷ INTENTION

▷ REFLECTION

AUG 21   SUNDAY

CARD OF THE DAY:

▷ INTENTION

▷ REFLECTION

AUG 22   MONDAY | *Happy Virgo Season!*   CARD OF THE DAY:

▷ INTENTION   ▷ REFLECTION

AUG 23   TUESDAY   CARD OF THE DAY:

▷ INTENTION   ▷ REFLECTION

AUG 24   WEDNESDAY   CARD OF THE DAY:

▷ INTENTION   ▷ REFLECTION

AUG 25   THURSDAY   CARD OF THE DAY:

▷ INTENTION   ▷ REFLECTION

AUG 26   FRIDAY   CARD OF THE DAY:

▷ INTENTION   ▷ REFLECTION

AUG 27   SATURDAY | ○ *New Moon in Virgo*   CARD OF THE DAY:

▷ INTENTION   ▷ REFLECTION

AUG 28   SUNDAY   CARD OF THE DAY:

▷ INTENTION   ▷ REFLECTION

AUG 29 MONDAY

CARD OF THE DAY:

▷ INTENTION

▷ REFLECTION

AUG 30 TUESDAY

CARD OF THE DAY:

▷ INTENTION

▷ REFLECTION

AUG 31 WEDNESDAY

CARD OF THE DAY:

▷ INTENTION

▷ REFLECTION

INSIGHTS

SEPTEMBER

THE EMPRESS

The Empress welcomes you with abundant, creative, and fertile energy in September. The time is ripe to bring your next big project to fruition. Ask yourself, "What am I creating and nurturing? What can I birth into the world?" You may have a new creative project, a business idea, or a personal commitment — something that started as a tiny seed and is now ready to be launched into the world. You are in a period of growth, in which all you have dreamed of is now coming to fruition. Your creativity is also closely aligned to the beauty you see around you. So, take a moment to find beauty in all things, no matter how small or ordinary, and use it to inspire your creative projects.

 RITUAL: BRING YOUR CREATIVE IDEA INTO FRUITION

This month is perfect for bringing your creative ideas into fruition, whether it's an art project, a new business, a new course, or a new health regime. Choose one idea that really gets your creative juices flowing and lights you up from the inside out. Then, every day for the month of September (and longer if you feel called), do at least one thing to bring your idea into being. For an extra creative boost, meditate with The Empress card each day and invite her to bring her energy into your daily routine.

 CRYSTAL: MOSS AGATE

Moss Agate supports and promotes physical well-being, and can help to balance the physical impact of your external environment. Moss Agate also helps us to see things from a fresh new perspective, making it an ideal stone for stimulating new ideas, self-expression, and communication.

ASTROLOGICAL INFLUENCES

September 9–October 2 | Mercury Retrograde:
Utilize the Tarot Reader's Survival Guide for Mercury Retrograde inside of your Toolkit www.biddytarot.com/2022-planner-bonus to help navigate through this time.

September 18 | Mercury opposite Jupiter: Be careful not to make promises you can't keep, or blow things out of proportion. Ensure your arguments are well thought out and backed by fact, rather than conjecture. Dot your i's and cross your t's.

September 22 | Happy Libra Season!
Balance, objectivity, fairness, aesthetics, charm.

INSIGHTS

SEPTEMBER 10

FULL MOON IN PISCES

A dreamy Full Moon in Pisces can intensify your connection to spirit and your intuition. Celebrate the manifestation of your imaginings and release any wishful thinking that isn't serving you now.

1. Which areas of my life have benefited most from my intuition?

2. What do I need to release in order to connect with myself on a deeper level?

3. Where do I need to focus more gratitude in the next six months?

4. What limiting beliefs must I release to expand my creative projects?

5. What can I focus on to deepen my spiritual practice?

6. How might the arts inspire my own creative success moving forward?

INSIGHTS

SEPTEMBER 25
NEW MOON
IN LIBRA

A New Moon in Libra is a beautiful time to explore your personal values and the environment and relationships that support you in feeling balanced.

1. Where in my life would I benefit most from a deeper sense of harmony?

2. How might evaluating my personal style have a positive impact on my life?

3. How can I create more beauty in my environment?

4. Where would I benefit from a more peaceful approach?

5. How can I bond more strongly with others?

6. What is my true intention in my current or future relationship?

INSIGHTS

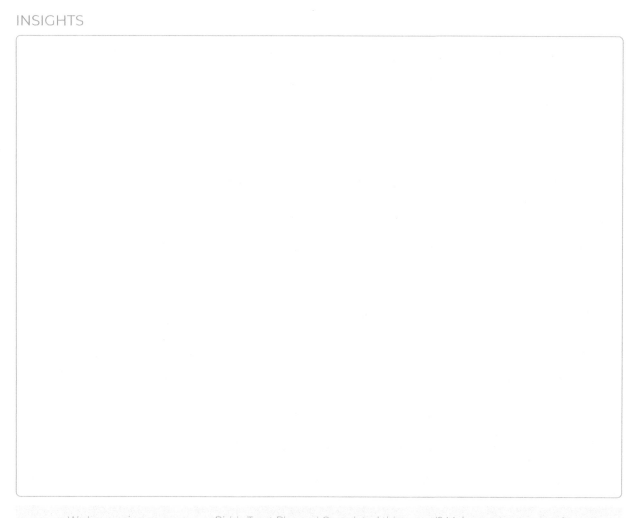

SEP 01 THURSDAY   CARD OF THE DAY:

▷ INTENTION   ▷ REFLECTION

SEP 02 FRIDAY   CARD OF THE DAY:

▷ INTENTION   ▷ REFLECTION

SEP 03 SATURDAY   CARD OF THE DAY:

▷ INTENTION   ▷ REFLECTION

SEP 04 SUNDAY   CARD OF THE DAY:

▷ INTENTION   ▷ REFLECTION

SEP 05 MONDAY   CARD OF THE DAY:

▷ INTENTION   ▷ REFLECTION

SEP 06 TUESDAY   CARD OF THE DAY:

▷ INTENTION   ▷ REFLECTION

SEP 07 WEDNESDAY   CARD OF THE DAY:

▷ INTENTION   ▷ REFLECTION

SEP 08 THURSDAY CARD OF THE DAY:

▷ INTENTION ▷ REFLECTION

SEP 09 FRIDAY | *Mercury Retrograde begins* CARD OF THE DAY:

▷ INTENTION ▷ REFLECTION

SEP 10 SATURDAY | ● *Full Moon in Pisces* CARD OF THE DAY:

▷ INTENTION ▷ REFLECTION

SEP 11 SUNDAY CARD OF THE DAY:

▷ INTENTION ▷ REFLECTION

SEP 12 MONDAY CARD OF THE DAY:

▷ INTENTION ▷ REFLECTION

SEP 13 TUESDAY CARD OF THE DAY:

▷ INTENTION ▷ REFLECTION

SEP 14 WEDNESDAY CARD OF THE DAY:

▷ INTENTION ▷ REFLECTION

SEP 15   THURSDAY   CARD OF THE DAY:

▷ INTENTION   ▷ REFLECTION

SEP 16   FRIDAY   CARD OF THE DAY:

▷ INTENTION   ▷ REFLECTION

SEP 17   SATURDAY   CARD OF THE DAY:

▷ INTENTION   ▷ REFLECTION

SEP 18   SUNDAY | *Mercury opposite Jupiter*   CARD OF THE DAY:

▷ INTENTION   ▷ REFLECTION

SEP 19   MONDAY   CARD OF THE DAY:

▷ INTENTION   ▷ REFLECTION

SEP 20   TUESDAY   CARD OF THE DAY:

▷ INTENTION   ▷ REFLECTION

SEP 21   WEDNESDAY   CARD OF THE DAY:

▷ INTENTION   ▷ REFLECTION

SEP 22　THURSDAY | *Happy Libra Season!*　CARD OF THE DAY:

▷ INTENTION

▷ REFLECTION

SEP 23　FRIDAY　CARD OF THE DAY:

▷ INTENTION

▷ REFLECTION

SEP 24　SATURDAY　CARD OF THE DAY:

▷ INTENTION

▷ REFLECTION

SEP 25　SUNDAY | ○ *New Moon in Libra*　CARD OF THE DAY:

▷ INTENTION

▷ REFLECTION

SEP 26　MONDAY　CARD OF THE DAY:

▷ INTENTION

▷ REFLECTION

SEP 27　TUESDAY　CARD OF THE DAY:

▷ INTENTION

▷ REFLECTION

SEP 28　WEDNESDAY　CARD OF THE DAY:

▷ INTENTION

▷ REFLECTION

SEP 29 THURSDAY   CARD OF THE DAY:

▷ INTENTION   ▷ REFLECTION

SEP 30 FRIDAY   CARD OF THE DAY:

▷ INTENTION   ▷ REFLECTION

INSIGHTS

FALL EQUINOX SPREAD

The Fall Equinox (September 22, 6:03 p.m. PT; March 20, 2:33 a.m. AEST) is the time of harvest. After the abundance of the Summer, it's time to reap what you've sown, celebrate with deep appreciation, then bunker down for the Winter season. This is the perfect time for slowing down, expressing gratitude for what you've achieved, and gathering your resources for the Winter period.

Use the following Tarot spread around the Fall Equinox to connect with this sacred energy.

1. What have I achieved during the Summer period?

2. What is the bounty of my harvest?

3. What am I truly grateful for?

4. What resources are available to me now?

5. What resources do I need to gather?

6. What can I release and let go?

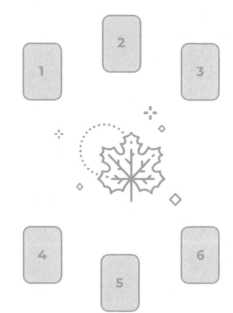

INSIGHTS

INSIGHTS

FALL EQUINOX INTENTIONS

Holding the energy and insight of your Fall Equinox Tarot Reading, set your intentions for the next three months:

OCTOBER

THE HIEROPHANT

With the help of The Hierophant, this month you have the opportunity to learn from a wise teacher who nurtures your spiritual awareness and helps you access the Divine by understanding its traditions and core principles. This teacher may appear as a coach, mentor, guru, author, spiritual leader, friend, or partner. Be open to receive their tried and tested advice about what does and doesn't work, and tap into their core beliefs, mindset, and philosophies, as these will guide you along your personal path. You may also find yourself not only in the student role, but that of the teacher, sharing your own wisdom with others and being a beacon of light and inspiration.

 RITUAL: CALL IN YOUR TEACHERS

This ritual is designed for when you feel uncertain about what to do and need some extra advice or words of wisdom to provide clarity. In your mind's eye, call in the energy of a teacher or guide who you believe can help you. It might be someone you know or have met. Or it might be a great leader from another lifetime. Bring the energy of this teacher to mind. Then ask for advice and wisdom to help you navigate the situation and find a solution. With a pen and paper, write down everything that comes to you, as if the teacher's advice is flowing through you. When you feel complete, thank the teacher for their guidance.

 CRYSTAL: LARIMAR

This crystal supports inner wisdom and manifestation, encouraging peace, harmony, and clarity of vision. For this reason, Larimar can also be used during times of great stress, panic or fear. Wear or use Larimar in your Tarot readings to support physical, emotional, mental, and spiritual release and healing.

 ASTROLOGICAL INFLUENCES

October 1 | Venus opposite Jupiter: Grab your dancing shoes and whirl into holiday season. But don't forget to check important things off your list first. Be mindful not to overspend on last-minute frivolities. Be careful not to appear too careless.

October 13 | Venus trine Saturn: Saturn brings a "grown up" and stabilizing influence to love. New relationships feel steadier, and mature relationships find a new sense of realism. Ask a mature role model for relationship advice.

October 23 | Happy Scorpio Season!
Transformation, intensity, ambition, control, reflection.

INSIGHTS

OCTOBER 9

FULL MOON IN ARIES

Honor your inner warrior with the Full Moon in Aries. Celebrate the ways you've grown into your strength, and release the fears that hold you back.

1. Where would I benefit most from being more fearless?

2. How can I release stress in a more constructive way?

3. Which battle is it time to release attachment to?

4. Where do I most need to be a little more selfish?

5. What do I need to release to be able to feel strong?

6. How can I be more compassionate toward others?

INSIGHTS

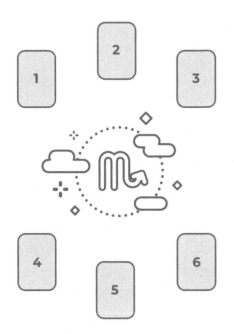

OCTOBER 25 | SOLAR ECLIPSE
NEW MOON IN SCORPIO

The New Moon in Scorpio is the ideal time to make conscious decisions about your spiritual transformation. Use this time to set your intentions about who you're becoming.

1. Which area of my life might experience the deepest transformation in the next six months?

2. How can I healthily express my deepest desires?

3. Which elements of my shadow self need some attention and care?

4. How can I release the desire to control or manipulate outcomes?

5. Where am I not being truly honest with myself?

6. How can I foster a deeper connection with my spiritual truth?

INSIGHTS

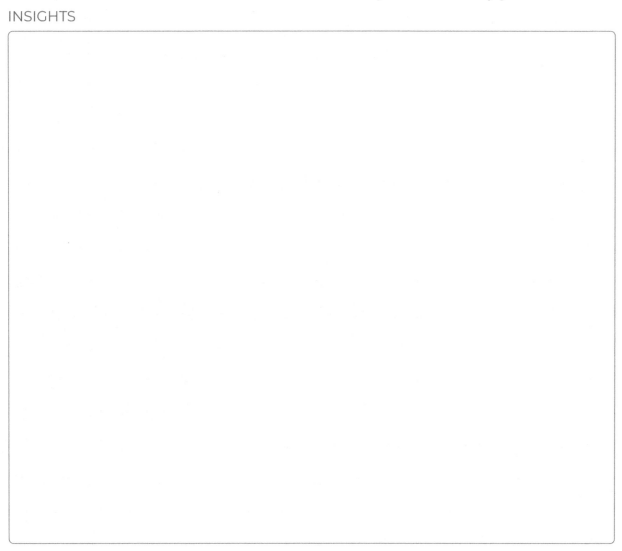

OCT 01 SATURDAY | *Venus opposite Jupiter*   CARD OF THE DAY:

▷ INTENTION   ▷ REFLECTION

OCT 02 SUNDAY | *Mercury Retrograde ends*   CARD OF THE DAY:

▷ INTENTION   ▷ REFLECTION

OCT 03 MONDAY   CARD OF THE DAY:

▷ INTENTION   ▷ REFLECTION

OCT 04 TUESDAY   CARD OF THE DAY:

▷ INTENTION   ▷ REFLECTION

OCT 05 WEDNESDAY   CARD OF THE DAY:

▷ INTENTION   ▷ REFLECTION

OCT 06 THURSDAY   CARD OF THE DAY:

▷ INTENTION   ▷ REFLECTION

OCT 07 FRIDAY   CARD OF THE DAY:

▷ INTENTION   ▷ REFLECTION

OCT 08 SATURDAY

CARD OF THE DAY:

▷ INTENTION

▷ REFLECTION

OCT 09 SUNDAY | ● *Full Moon in Aries*

CARD OF THE DAY:

▷ INTENTION

▷ REFLECTION

OCT 10 MONDAY

CARD OF THE DAY:

▷ INTENTION

▷ REFLECTION

OCT 11 TUESDAY

CARD OF THE DAY:

▷ INTENTION

▷ REFLECTION

OCT 12 WEDNESDAY

CARD OF THE DAY:

▷ INTENTION

▷ REFLECTION

OCT 13 THURSDAY | *Venus trine Saturn*

CARD OF THE DAY:

▷ INTENTION

▷ REFLECTION

OCT 14 FRIDAY

CARD OF THE DAY:

▷ INTENTION

▷ REFLECTION

OCT 15 SATURDAY   CARD OF THE DAY:

▷ INTENTION   ▷ REFLECTION

OCT 16 SUNDAY   CARD OF THE DAY:

▷ INTENTION   ▷ REFLECTION

OCT 17 MONDAY   CARD OF THE DAY:

▷ INTENTION   ▷ REFLECTION

OCT 18 TUESDAY   CARD OF THE DAY:

▷ INTENTION   ▷ REFLECTION

OCT 19 WEDNESDAY   CARD OF THE DAY:

▷ INTENTION   ▷ REFLECTION

OCT 20 THURSDAY   CARD OF THE DAY:

▷ INTENTION   ▷ REFLECTION

OCT 21 FRIDAY   CARD OF THE DAY:

▷ INTENTION   ▷ REFLECTION

OCT 22   SATURDAY

CARD OF THE DAY:

▷ INTENTION

▷ REFLECTION

OCT 23   SUNDAY | *Happy Scorpio Season!*

CARD OF THE DAY:

▷ INTENTION

▷ REFLECTION

OCT 24   MONDAY

CARD OF THE DAY:

▷ INTENTION

▷ REFLECTION

OCT 25   TUESDAY | ○ *New Moon in Scorpio*

CARD OF THE DAY:

▷ INTENTION

▷ REFLECTION

OCT 26   WEDNESDAY

CARD OF THE DAY:

▷ INTENTION

▷ REFLECTION

OCT 27   THURSDAY

CARD OF THE DAY:

▷ INTENTION

▷ REFLECTION

OCT 28   FRIDAY

CARD OF THE DAY:

▷ INTENTION

▷ REFLECTION

OCT 29 SATURDAY CARD OF THE DAY:

▷ INTENTION   ▷ REFLECTION

OCT 30 SUNDAY CARD OF THE DAY:

▷ INTENTION   ▷ REFLECTION

OCT 31 MONDAY CARD OF THE DAY:

▷ INTENTION   ▷ REFLECTION

INSIGHTS

NOVEMBER

THE MOON

With the energy of The Moon, November is the month for the deep, intuitive work your soul is craving right now. Pull out your crystals, candles, and Tarot cards, and pay attention to the subtle cues and symbols that are all around you. Messages are aplenty but you need to be tuned in to the collective energy to recognize and interpret them. Make spiritual self-care your priority and you'll reap the benefits. This is also the perfect time to tune into the moon cycles and make them a part of your life's flow. Connect with the divine feminine and uncover deep intuitive insights and visions of what lies beyond everyday life.

⚘ RITUAL: HONORING THE MOON CYCLES

This month, you are invited to honor the moon cycles and integrate them into your life's flow and natural rhythm. On the New Moon, set your intentions for growth and expansion for the next two weeks. And on the Full Moon, give thanks for what you have created, then release what no longer serves you. If you wish to go deeper, see the Planner Toolkit for the complete Moon Rituals.

⚗ CRYSTAL: BLACK ONYX

A powerful stone of protection, Black Onyx absorbs and transforms negative energy. Wear or keep Black Onyx close by during your Tarot readings to prevent becoming drained. Black Onyx also encourages your truest nature, allowing others to more easily access the depths of who you really are.

🪐 ASTROLOGICAL INFLUENCES

November 10 | Venus trine Neptune: This is a time for romance, compassion, and kindness. A magical transit to connect with others and express creativity. You may have a tendency to romanticize — but be wary of rosy-colored red flags.

November 17 | Mercury into Sagittarius: This transit brings an expansion of thinking. It helps us become more open-minded — less concerned by details, and open to discussing new ideas. Be considerate of others and stick to the truth.

November 22 | Happy Sagittarius Season!
Adventure, optimism, philosophy, honesty, travel.

INSIGHTS

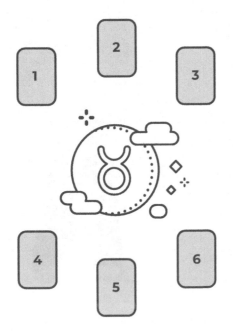

NOVEMBER 8 | LUNAR ECLIPSE
FULL MOON IN TAURUS

The Taurus Full Moon Lunar Eclipse brings the focus to your physical resources and sense of peace. Luxuriate in sensual pleasures and release anything that feels like drama.

1. Which resources that I have gathered in the past six months will bring me the most joy?

2. What can I do to inspire more serenity in my life?

3. What do I need to do to feel more physically grounded?

4. How can I achieve a sense of absolute presence in my relationships?

5. What can I let go of now to make life feel easy?

6. How might my current or future relationship benefit from better understanding my sensuality?

INSIGHTS

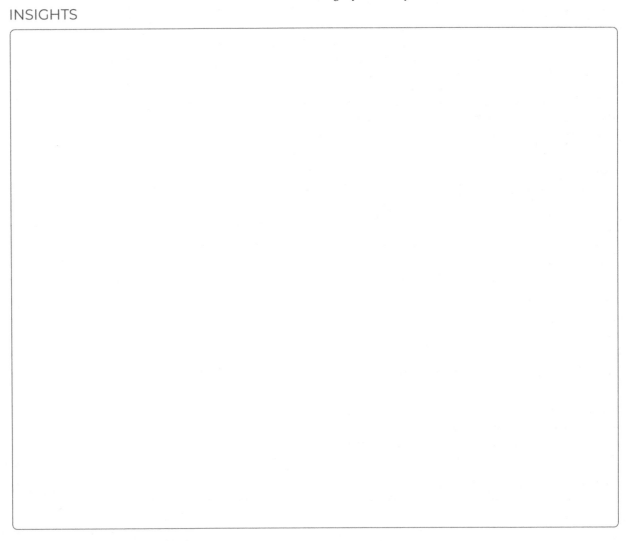

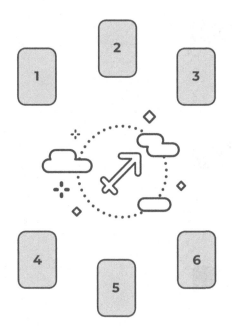

NOVEMBER 23

NEW MOON IN SAGITTARIUS

The New Moon in Sagittarius encourages you to expand your awareness and perspective. Set intentions around adventures and experiences that will broaden your worldview.

1. Where do I need to focus on expanding my awareness?

2. What can I do to inspire a sense of adventure in my life?

3. What can I do to expand my friendship circles and connect with new people?

4. What is my ideal vision for the global community?

5. What lessons have I learned from travel in the past six months?

6. How can I utilize those lessons to inspire others?

INSIGHTS

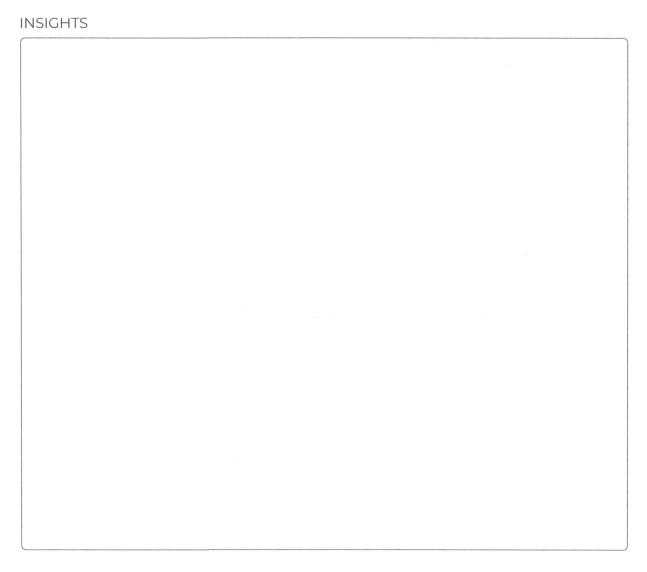

NOV 01 TUESDAY

CARD OF THE DAY:

▷ INTENTION

▷ REFLECTION

NOV 02 WEDNESDAY

CARD OF THE DAY:

▷ INTENTION

▷ REFLECTION

NOV 03 THURSDAY

CARD OF THE DAY:

▷ INTENTION

▷ REFLECTION

NOV 04 FRIDAY

CARD OF THE DAY:

▷ INTENTION

▷ REFLECTION

NOV 05 SATURDAY

CARD OF THE DAY:

▷ INTENTION

▷ REFLECTION

NOV 06 SUNDAY

CARD OF THE DAY:

▷ INTENTION

▷ REFLECTION

NOV 07 MONDAY

CARD OF THE DAY:

▷ INTENTION

▷ REFLECTION

NOV 08 TUESDAY | ● *Full Moon in Taurus*   CARD OF THE DAY:

▷ INTENTION

▷ REFLECTION

NOV 09 WEDNESDAY   CARD OF THE DAY:

▷ INTENTION

▷ REFLECTION

NOV 10 THURSDAY | *Venus trine Neptune*   CARD OF THE DAY:

▷ INTENTION

▷ REFLECTION

NOV 11 FRIDAY   CARD OF THE DAY:

▷ INTENTION

▷ REFLECTION

NOV 12 SATURDAY   CARD OF THE DAY:

▷ INTENTION

▷ REFLECTION

NOV 13 SUNDAY   CARD OF THE DAY:

▷ INTENTION

▷ REFLECTION

NOV 14 MONDAY   CARD OF THE DAY:

▷ INTENTION

▷ REFLECTION

NOV 15 — TUESDAY
CARD OF THE DAY:

▷ INTENTION

▷ REFLECTION

NOV 16 — WEDNESDAY
CARD OF THE DAY:

▷ INTENTION

▷ REFLECTION

NOV 17 — THURSDAY | *Mercury into Sagittarius*
CARD OF THE DAY:

▷ INTENTION

▷ REFLECTION

NOV 18 — FRIDAY
CARD OF THE DAY:

▷ INTENTION

▷ REFLECTION

NOV 19 — SATURDAY
CARD OF THE DAY:

▷ INTENTION

▷ REFLECTION

NOV 20 — SUNDAY
CARD OF THE DAY:

▷ INTENTION

▷ REFLECTION

NOV 21 — MONDAY
CARD OF THE DAY:

▷ INTENTION

▷ REFLECTION

NOV 22 TUESDAY | *Happy Sagittarius Season!* CARD OF THE DAY:

▷ INTENTION   ▷ REFLECTION

NOV 23 WEDNESDAY | ○ *New Moon in Sagittarius* CARD OF THE DAY:

▷ INTENTION   ▷ REFLECTION

NOV 24 THURSDAY   CARD OF THE DAY:

▷ INTENTION   ▷ REFLECTION

NOV 25 FRIDAY   CARD OF THE DAY:

▷ INTENTION   ▷ REFLECTION

NOV 26 SATURDAY   CARD OF THE DAY:

▷ INTENTION   ▷ REFLECTION

NOV 27 SUNDAY   CARD OF THE DAY:

▷ INTENTION   ▷ REFLECTION

NOV 28 MONDAY   CARD OF THE DAY:

▷ INTENTION   ▷ REFLECTION

NOV 29 TUESDAY   CARD OF THE DAY:

▷ INTENTION   ▷ REFLECTION

NOV 30 WEDNESDAY   CARD OF THE DAY:

▷ INTENTION   ▷ REFLECTION

INSIGHTS

DECEMBER

THE HANGED MAN

As the year comes to a close, The Hanged Man is calling on you to slow down, surrender, and hit pause on your regular routine this month. You might like to take a creative break, where you can replenish your energy and let your creative juices flow in your own time and space. This is your invitation to see the world from a different perspective and embrace new opportunities that will only become apparent once you slow down enough to see them. You may also be inspired (or forced) to put important projects on hold, even if it is completely inconvenient to do so. Don't keep pushing forward, hoping that more action will drive you to where you want to go. Instead, surrender to the opportunity to pause and view it as your chance to reassess and re-evaluate where you are on your path.

 ### RITUAL: RELEASE AND LET GO

Find a place outside where you can lie on the ground and not be disturbed. Before that, find The Hanged Man in your favorite deck and draw in the energy of this powerful card. Then, lay yourself down comfortably on the ground. Feel yourself relax, and as you slowly let go and surrender, feel the earth supporting you. Then, look up into the sky and notice how different it looks from this perspective. Notice the clouds passing by in different shapes, and the gradients of color reaching out into the Universe. Take three long, deep breaths, and notice how comfortably the earth holds you. As you breathe out, feel your body, mind, and soul release anything that no longer serves you into the wide, open sky. When you're ready, slowly rise and write your insights into your Planner.

 ### CRYSTAL: AVENTURINE

Aventurine is a beautiful stone to promote joy, gratitude, and abundance. Known for opening the heart chakra, Aventurine helps us to give and receive love freely. Aventurine also helps to stimulate creativity, making it a wonderful stone to keep on hand when designing your own Tarot spreads, or working on your Tarot journal.

 ### ASTROLOGICAL INFLUENCES

December 20 | Jupiter into Aries: Fire up with new beginnings, while Jupiter swings into Aries! Let go of the past, get excited, and charge forward with purpose. Have fun exploring who it is you truly want to be.

December 21 | Happy Capricorn Season!
Persistence, realism, practicality, sensitivity, discipline.

December 29–January 18, 2023 | Mercury Retrograde: Utilize the Tarot Reader's Survival Guide for Mercury Retrograde inside of your Toolkit at www.biddytarot.com/2022-planner-bonus to help navigate through this time.

INSIGHTS

DECEMBER 7

FULL MOON
IN GEMINI

The Full Moon in Gemini enhances your vitality and brings to light the ways you perceive the world. Release any feelings of boredom and explore your curiosities.

1. How have my perceptions of the world changed in the last six months?

2. What new information have I learned that I can now teach others?

3. How has verbalizing my emotions impacted my closest relationships this year?

4. What valuable lessons have I learned from others?

5. What valuable lessons have I been able to teach others?

6. How can I approach problems in a more logical and calculated way?

INSIGHTS

DECEMBER 23
NEW MOON IN CAPRICORN

The last New Moon of the year falls in Capricorn, which rules stability, structure, and goals. It's a great time to work on a solid plan that will bring your dreams to life in 2023.

1. What insights did I gain in 2022 around what I want to achieve in 2023?

2. Which areas of my life might benefit from creating a sense of order?

3. How can I best support my financial goals this year?

4. What goals do I want to achieve within the next six months?

5. What kind of structure do I need to establish to support those goals?

6. Which grounding practices would best support me this year?

INSIGHTS

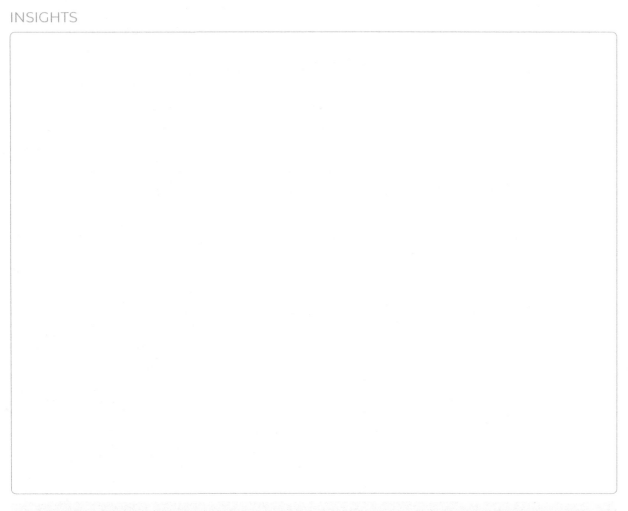

DEC 01 THURSDAY   CARD OF THE DAY:

▷ INTENTION   ▷ REFLECTION

DEC 02 FRIDAY   CARD OF THE DAY:

▷ INTENTION   ▷ REFLECTION

DEC 03 SATURDAY   CARD OF THE DAY:

▷ INTENTION   ▷ REFLECTION

DEC 04 SUNDAY   CARD OF THE DAY:

▷ INTENTION   ▷ REFLECTION

DEC 05 MONDAY   CARD OF THE DAY:

▷ INTENTION   ▷ REFLECTION

DEC 06 TUESDAY   CARD OF THE DAY:

▷ INTENTION   ▷ REFLECTION

DEC 07 WEDNESDAY | ● *Full Moon in Gemini*   CARD OF THE DAY:

▷ INTENTION   ▷ REFLECTION

DEC 08 THURSDAY CARD OF THE DAY:

▷ INTENTION ▷ REFLECTION

DEC 09 FRIDAY CARD OF THE DAY:

▷ INTENTION ▷ REFLECTION

DEC 10 SATURDAY CARD OF THE DAY:

▷ INTENTION ▷ REFLECTION

DEC 11 SUNDAY CARD OF THE DAY:

▷ INTENTION ▷ REFLECTION

DEC 12 MONDAY CARD OF THE DAY:

▷ INTENTION ▷ REFLECTION

DEC 13 TUESDAY CARD OF THE DAY:

▷ INTENTION ▷ REFLECTION

DEC 14 WEDNESDAY CARD OF THE DAY:

▷ INTENTION ▷ REFLECTION

DEC 15 THURSDAY   CARD OF THE DAY:

▷ INTENTION   ▷ REFLECTION

DEC 16 FRIDAY   CARD OF THE DAY:

▷ INTENTION   ▷ REFLECTION

DEC 17 SATURDAY   CARD OF THE DAY:

▷ INTENTION   ▷ REFLECTION

DEC 18 SUNDAY   CARD OF THE DAY:

▷ INTENTION   ▷ REFLECTION

DEC 19 MONDAY   CARD OF THE DAY:

▷ INTENTION   ▷ REFLECTION

DEC 20 TUESDAY | *Jupiter into Aries*   CARD OF THE DAY:

▷ INTENTION   ▷ REFLECTION

DEC 21 WEDNESDAY | *Happy Capricorn Season!* CARD OF THE DAY:

▷ INTENTION   ▷ REFLECTION

DEC 22   THURSDAY

CARD OF THE DAY:

▷ INTENTION

▷ REFLECTION

DEC 23   FRIDAY | ○ New Moon in Capricorn

CARD OF THE DAY:

▷ INTENTION

▷ REFLECTION

DEC 24   SATURDAY

CARD OF THE DAY:

▷ INTENTION

▷ REFLECTION

DEC 25   SUNDAY

CARD OF THE DAY:

▷ INTENTION

▷ REFLECTION

DEC 26   MONDAY

CARD OF THE DAY:

▷ INTENTION

▷ REFLECTION

DEC 27   TUESDAY

CARD OF THE DAY:

▷ INTENTION

▷ REFLECTION

DEC 28   WEDNESDAY

CARD OF THE DAY:

▷ INTENTION

▷ REFLECTION

DEC 29 THURSDAY | *Mercury Retrograde begins*   CARD OF THE DAY:

▷ INTENTION   ▷ REFLECTION

DEC 30 FRIDAY   CARD OF THE DAY:

▷ INTENTION   ▷ REFLECTION

DEC 31 SATURDAY   CARD OF THE DAY:

▷ INTENTION   ▷ REFLECTION

INSIGHTS

WINTER SOLSTICE SPREAD

The Winter Solstice (December 21, 1:48 p.m. PT; June 21, 7:13 p.m. AEST), is the perfect time to go within, to step into the darkness and hibernate. It's time to reflect on your shadow self — the part of you that you try to deny or hide from others. Through this self-reflection, you'll emerge once again into the light as your most powerful self.

Use the following Tarot spread during the Winter Solstice to connect with this sacred energy.

1. What is the essence of my inner shadow self?

2. What can I learn from my shadow self?

3. How can I bring my shadow self into the light?

4. What lights me up from within?

5. What new seeds am I planting?

6. What do I need to release in order to create space for growth?

INSIGHTS

WINTER SOLSTICE INTENTIONS

Holding the energy and insight of your Winter Solstice Tarot Reading, set your intentions for the next three months:

2022 REFLECTION

As we come to the end of 2022, take some time to reflect on the past 12 months and prepare yourself for the year to come. Go back to the New Year's Tarot Spread you completed in January and reflect on what has emerged over the course of the year.

Then, go through the questions below and for each one, journal your intuitive thoughts first, then if you feel called to do so, draw a Tarot card to help you go deeper.

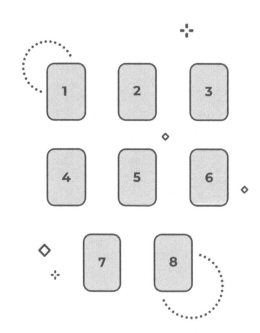

1. What were my biggest achievements for 2022?

2. What were my biggest challenges for 2022?

3. How have I developed as a person?

4. What did I learn in 2022?

5. How would I describe 2022 in just three words?

6. What is now complete?

7. What continues into 2023?

8. What new seeds and opportunities are being planted?

1. _____ FOR 2022?

```
        TRANSACTION RECORD

    Duke's Lake Union

CARD TYPE:MASTERCARD
Nu. ***********0153 EXPI.: ****
ENTRY:SWIPED
AUTHORIZATION:459899
STORE #:0
TERMINAL:6
REFERENCE:1209938

PURCHASE        $13.89

TIP          _____

TOTAL        _____

        THANK YOU
  AUGUST 1,2022 12:18:04
    Server's name : CIARRA

    CUSTOMER COPY
```

ur spread and your Tarot Planner with the
we'll share with the Biddy Tarot community!

2. WHAT WERE MY BIGGEST CHALLENGES FOR 2022?

3. HOW HAVE I DEVELOPED AS A PERSON?

4. WHAT DID I LEARN IN 2022?

5. HOW WOULD I DESCRIBE 2022 IN JUST THREE WORDS?

6. WHAT IS NOW COMPLETE?

7. WHAT CONTINUES INTO 2023?

8. WHAT NEW SEEDS AND OPPORTUNITIES ARE BEING PLANTED?

LEARN TO READ TAROT INTUITIVELY...

Access these Biddy Tarot learning resources to activate your intuition and reach YOUR highest potential. Learn more about these resources — and our full range of Tarot courses and programs — to help you on your journey at www.biddytarot.com/shop.

THE ULTIMATE GUIDE TO TAROT CARD MEANINGS
Fresh, Modern, Practical Guide To The Meanings Of Every Tarot Card

The *Ultimate Guide to Tarot Card Meanings* has everything you need to read the Tarot cards as simply as reading a magazine. Just imagine — all the Tarot card meanings you could ever want, right at your fingertips in this comprehensive, 400+ page reference guide. You'll never need to buy another book on Tarot card meanings again!

Available for purchase at www.biddytarot.com/guide.

INTUITIVE TAROT: 31 DAYS TO LEARN TO READ TAROT CARDS AND DEVELOP YOUR INTUITION
Trust Your Intuition, Access Your Inner Power, And Bring The Divine Into Your Everyday Life

With *Intuitive Tarot*, you can learn to access your intuition and confidently read the cards without a reference guide. Imagine the thrill of looking at a card (or even a full Tarot spread) and instantly understanding the message it has for you. Through 31 daily lessons and activities, you'll learn to quickly and accurately interpret the cards, and unlock the secrets to an insightful reading. It's already inside you — you just need to trust it.

Available for purchase at www.biddytarot.com/tarot-guides/intuitive-tarot.

TAROT 101
A Step-By-Step Beginner Video Series and Workbook for Tarot Lovers Everywhere

Do you want to learn to connect with the Tarot and trust your intuition? *Tarot 101* is the ultimate course for Tarot beginners eager to harness the powerful messages of the cards. The guided program features in-depth lessons, including steps on how to do readings with clarity and tell an accurate and insightful story with the cards. Are you ready to start your Tarot journey? Sign up for the *Tarot 101* program today!

Available for purchase at www.biddytarot.com/tarot-101-course.

MASTER THE TAROT
CARD MEANINGS

MASTER THE TAROT CARD MEANINGS PROGRAM

Stop Memorizing the Cards and Start Listening to Your Intuition

The *Master the Tarot Card Meanings* program will help you learn to read Tarot from your heart, not a book. Each lesson empowers you to build a unique personal connection with the Tarot, using simple yet powerful techniques for interpreting the cards. In just seven modules, you'll unlock the secrets of the Major and Minor Arcana, Court Cards, and reversed readings using Numerology, Symbolism, and so much more. By the end of the program, you'll have the power to intuitively access the meaning behind any spread!

Available for purchase at www.biddytarot.com/mtcm.

THE BIDDY TAROT COMMUNITY

Join a global, online community of 2000+ Tarot lovers and develop your Tarot reading skills

The Biddy Tarot Community is the only online community of its kind. Connect with 2,000+ Tarot lovers all over the world and get resources to help you learn and grow in your practice. Members get access to tons of Tarot resources, exclusive classes, the free Tarot reading platform to practice readings, and a unique TarotPath to help you level up on your Tarot journey.

Join the Biddy Tarot Community at www.biddytarot.com/community.